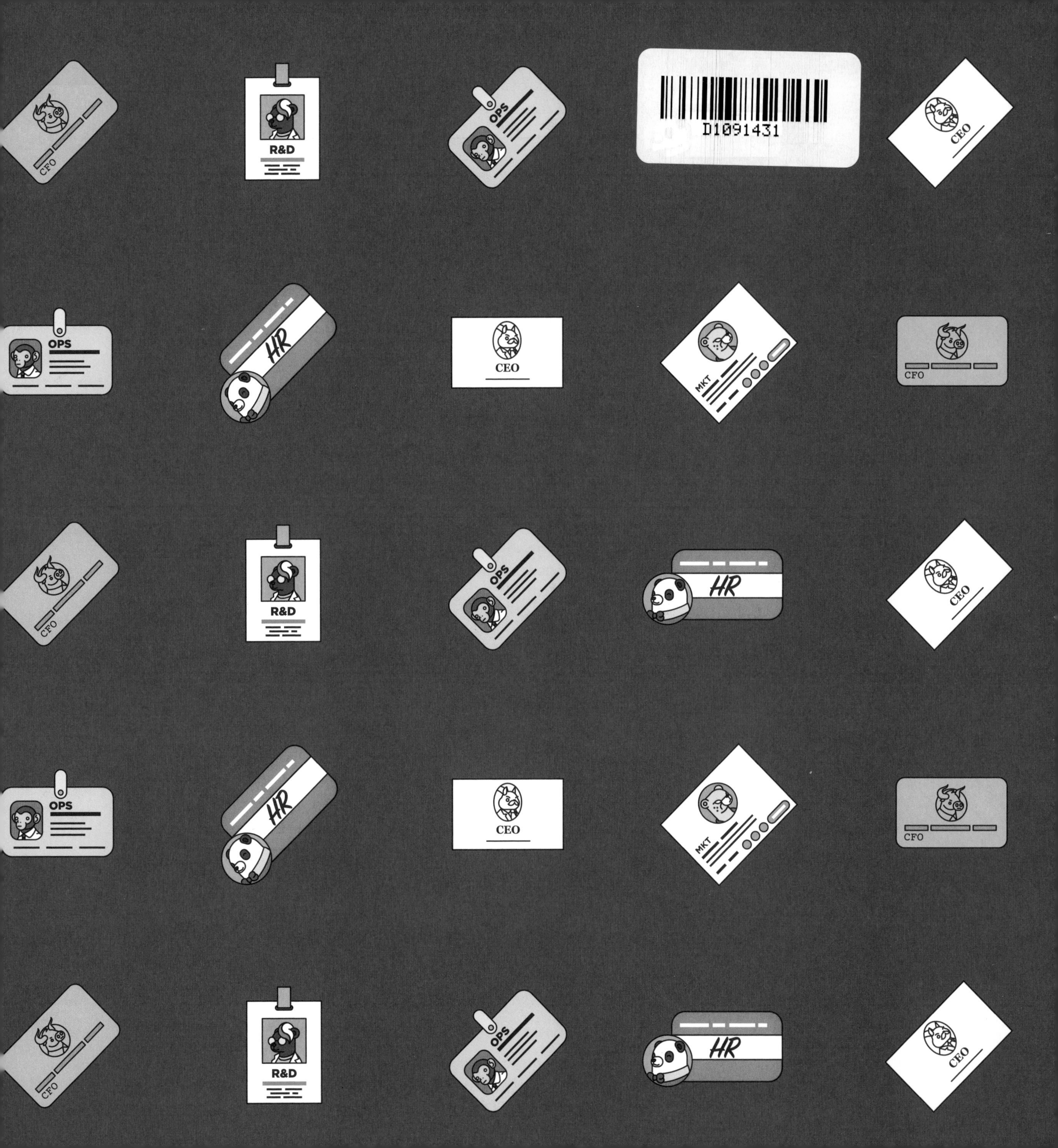
CFO
R&D
OPS
CEO
OPS
HR
CEO
MKT
CFO
CFO
R&D
OPS
HR
CEO
OPS
HR
CEO
MKT
CFO
CFO
R&D
OPS
HR
CEO

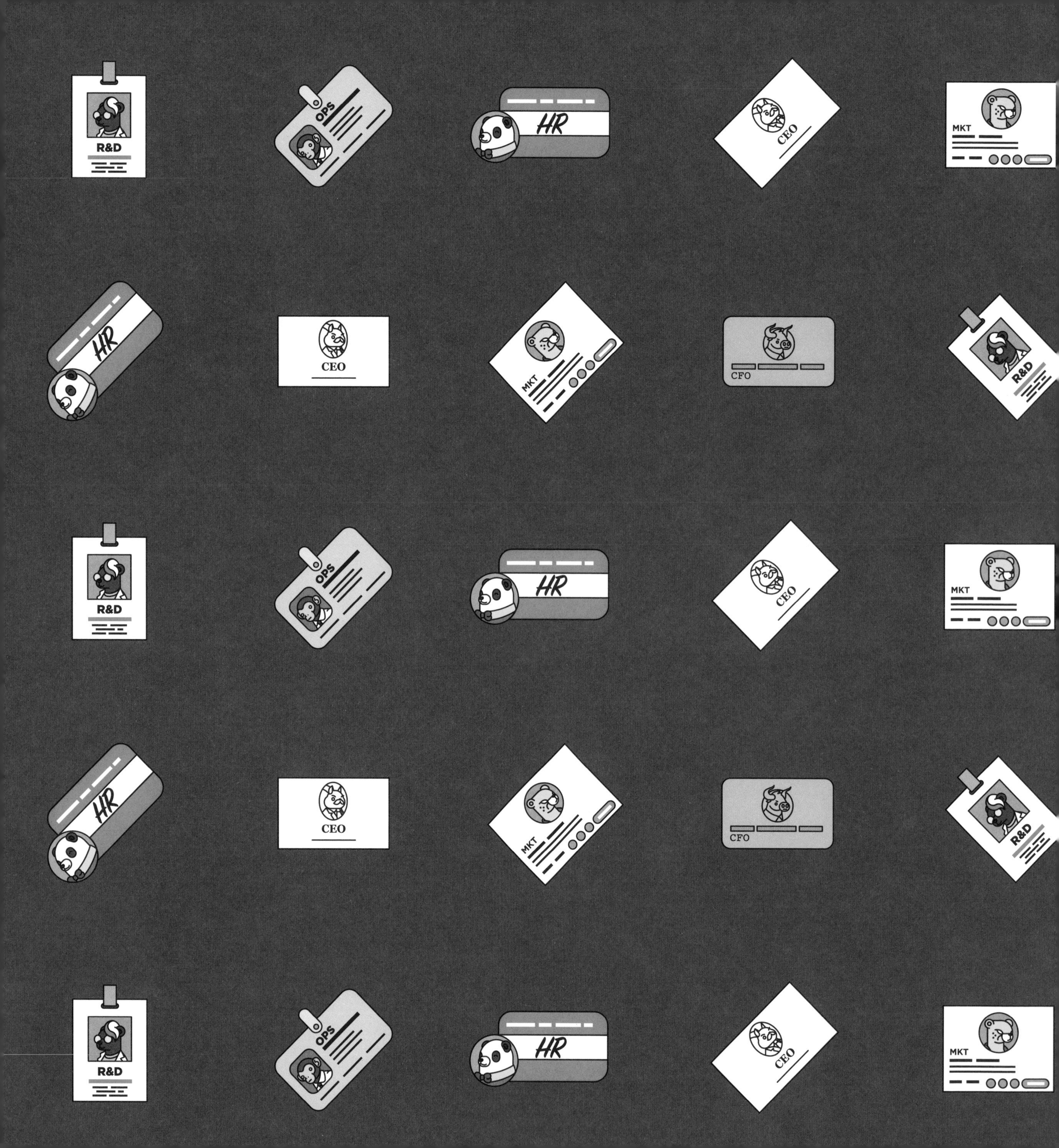
R&D
OPS
HR
CEO
MKT
HR
CEO
MKT
CFO
R&D
R&D
OPS
HR
CEO
MKT
HR
CEO
MKT
CFO
R&D
R&D
OPS
HR
CEO
MKT

WHAT IS STRATEGY?

An Illustrated Guide to Michael Porter

Written by Joan Magretta

Illustrated by Emile Holmewood | Conceived by Heinrich Zimmermann

HARVARD BUSINESS REVIEW PRESS

Boston, Massachusetts

AUTHOR NOTE: BEFORE YOU BEGIN

This is not your father's business book. It's aimed at readers in all types of organizations who learn visually as well as verbally. It's aimed at time-starved readers who want to absorb important content fast. It's aimed at readers who are serious about learning, but who also enjoy a good laugh. So we have created an imaginary management team aided by Michael Porter as they grapple with the challenges of strategy—and their own egos. The characters are fictional, but Porter's groundbreaking frameworks and the companies used to illustrate them are real.

For readers new to this graphic format, here's how to get the most out of this book.

1. First, read the page title—which tells you where you are in the story—and take a minute to enjoy the illustration.

2. Follow the back-and-forth between characters via the rectangular dialogue boxes. Read these from left to right on each page and not across each facing two-page spread.

3. White boxes with rounded corners feature text by the author. Read these in the order in which they appear.

4. The blue boxes highlight key takeaways. After you have read the whole book, you can easily refer back to these for a review of Porter's core concepts.

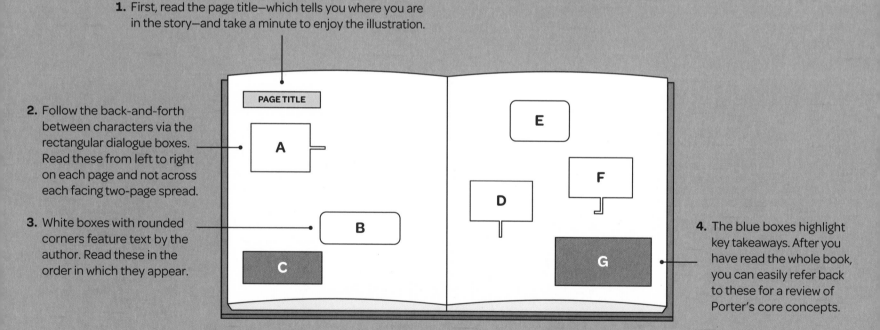

PAGE TITLE

A

B

C

D

E

F

G

5. Pause to take in the illustration before you turn the page.

TABLE OF CONTENTS

TODAY'S AGENDA:
COMPETITION AND STRATEGY

COMPETITION:

Before you can develop a good strategy, you need to get smart about how competition really works.

STRATEGY:

Once you're grounded in the economics of competition, you can test your current strategy or develop a new one.

Ready to get started? Imagine yourself as the proverbial fly on the wall at a strategy meeting led by me, Michael Porter. Turn the page and meet the executive team. Their meeting is about to begin…

THE EXECUTIVE TEAM HEADS TO THE BOARDROOM

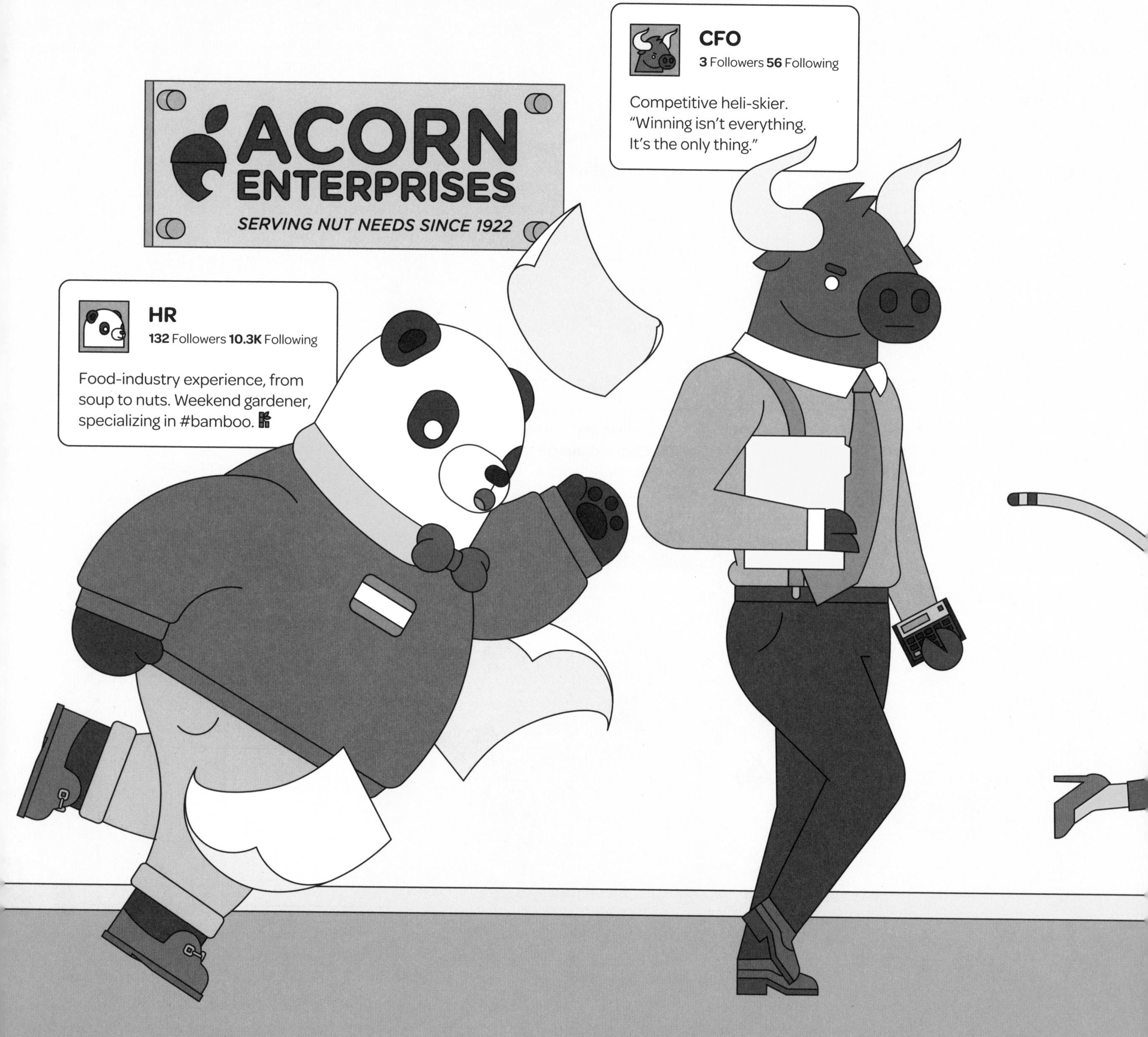
CFO
3 Followers 56 Following
Competitive heli-skier. “Winning isn’t everything. It’s the only thing.”
ACORN ENTERPRISES
SERVING NUT NEEDS SINCE 1922
HR
132 Followers 10.3K Following
Food-industry experience, from soup to nuts. Weekend gardener, specializing in #bamboo.

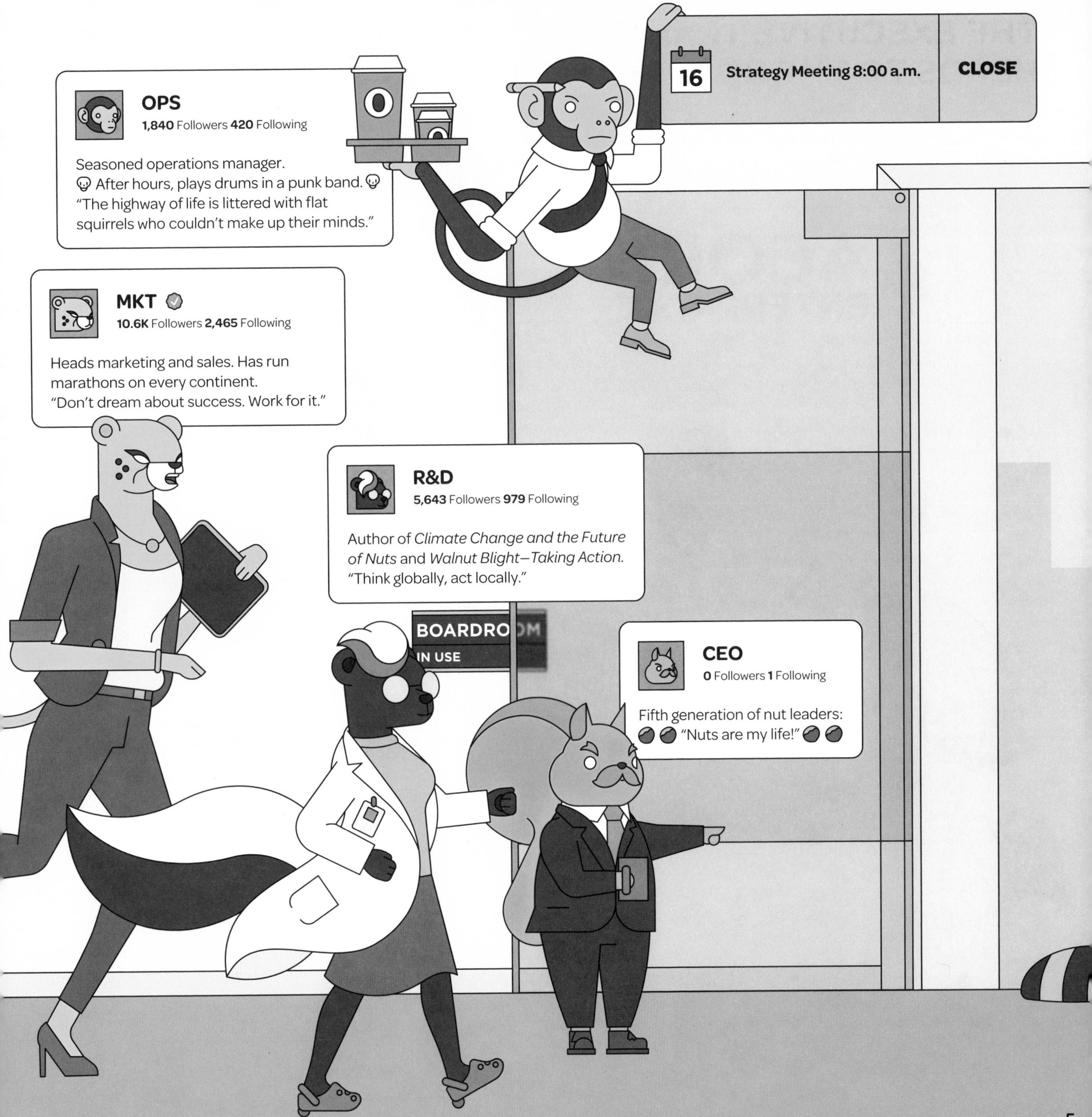
16
Strategy Meeting 8:00 a.m.
CLOSE
OPS
1,840 Followers 420 Following
Seasoned operations manager.
After hours, plays drums in a punk band.
"The highway of life is littered with flat squirrels who couldn't make up their minds."
MKT
10.6K Followers 2,465 Following
Heads marketing and sales. Has run marathons on every continent.
"Don't dream about success. Work for it."
R&D
5,643 Followers 979 Following
Author of *Climate Change and the Future of Nuts* and *Walnut Blight—Taking Action.*
"Think globally, act locally."
BOARDROOM
IN USE
CEO
0 Followers 1 Following
Fifth generation of nut leaders:
"Nuts are my life!"

BAD NEWS FROM THE CEO

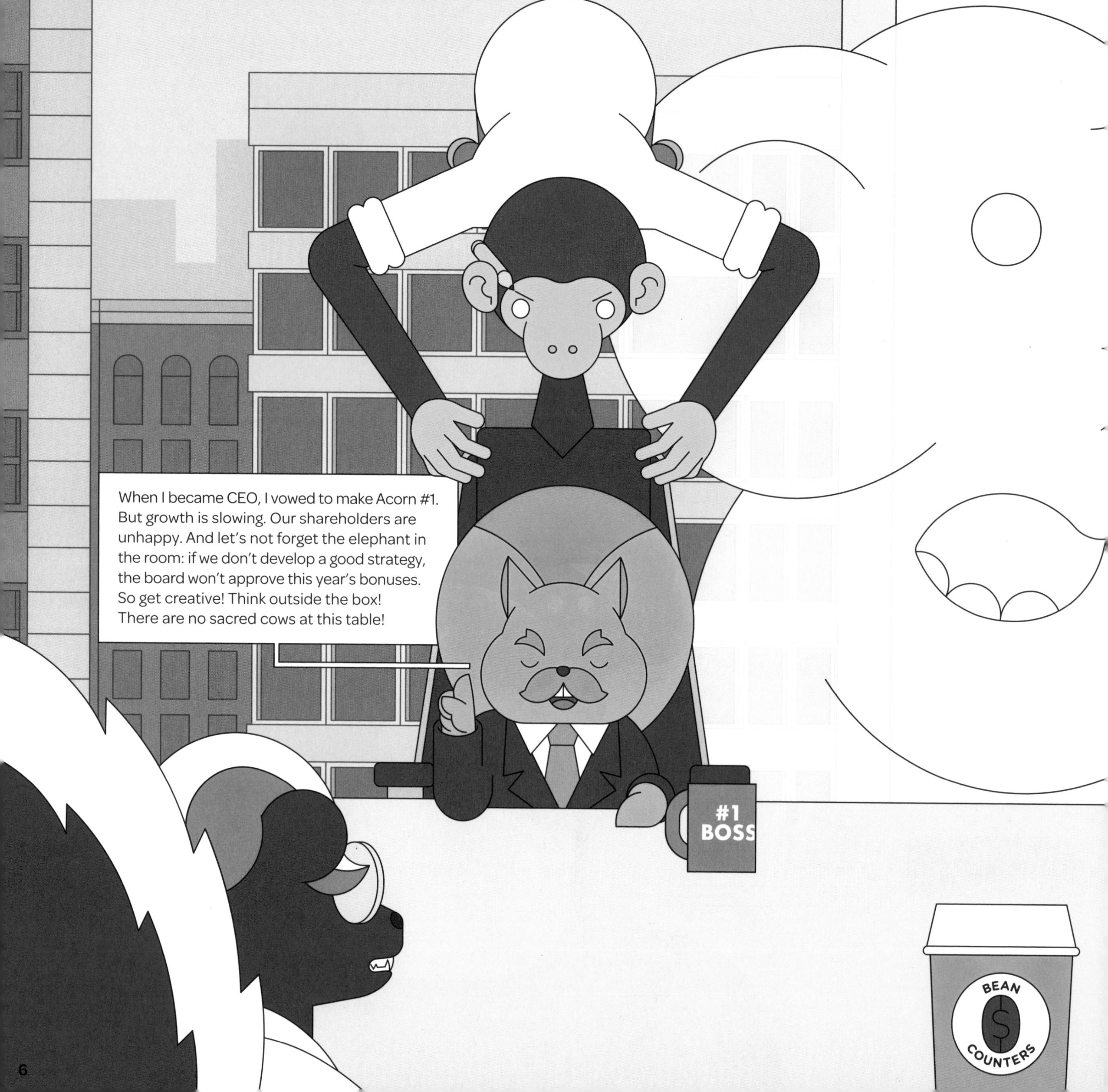
When I became CEO, I vowed to make Acorn #1. But growth is slowing. Our shareholders are unhappy. And let's not forget the elephant in the room: if we don't develop a good strategy, the board won't approve this year's bonuses. So get creative! Think outside the box! There are no sacred cows at this table!
#1 BOSS
BEAN COUNTERS

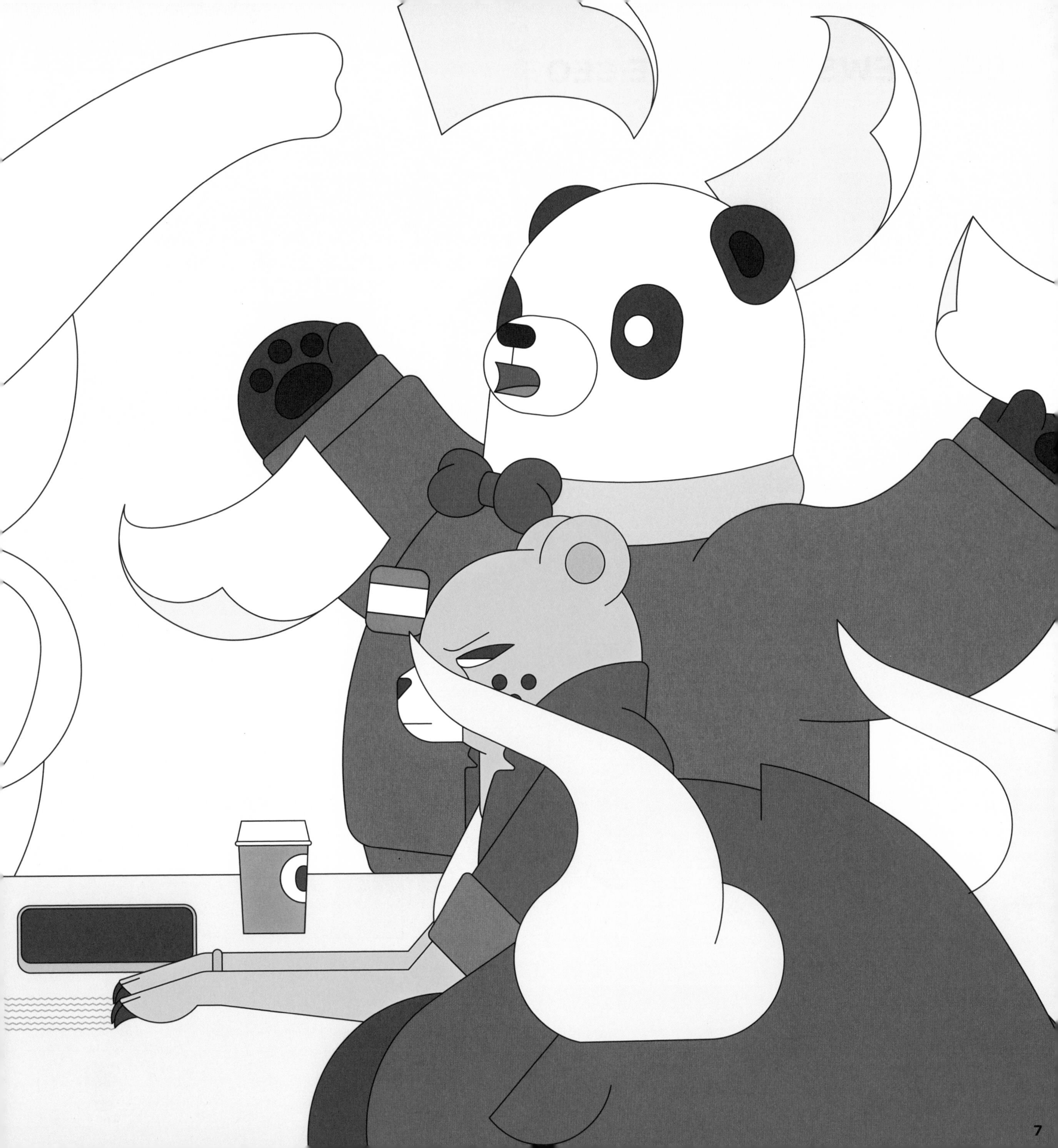

THE MEETING DRAGS ON

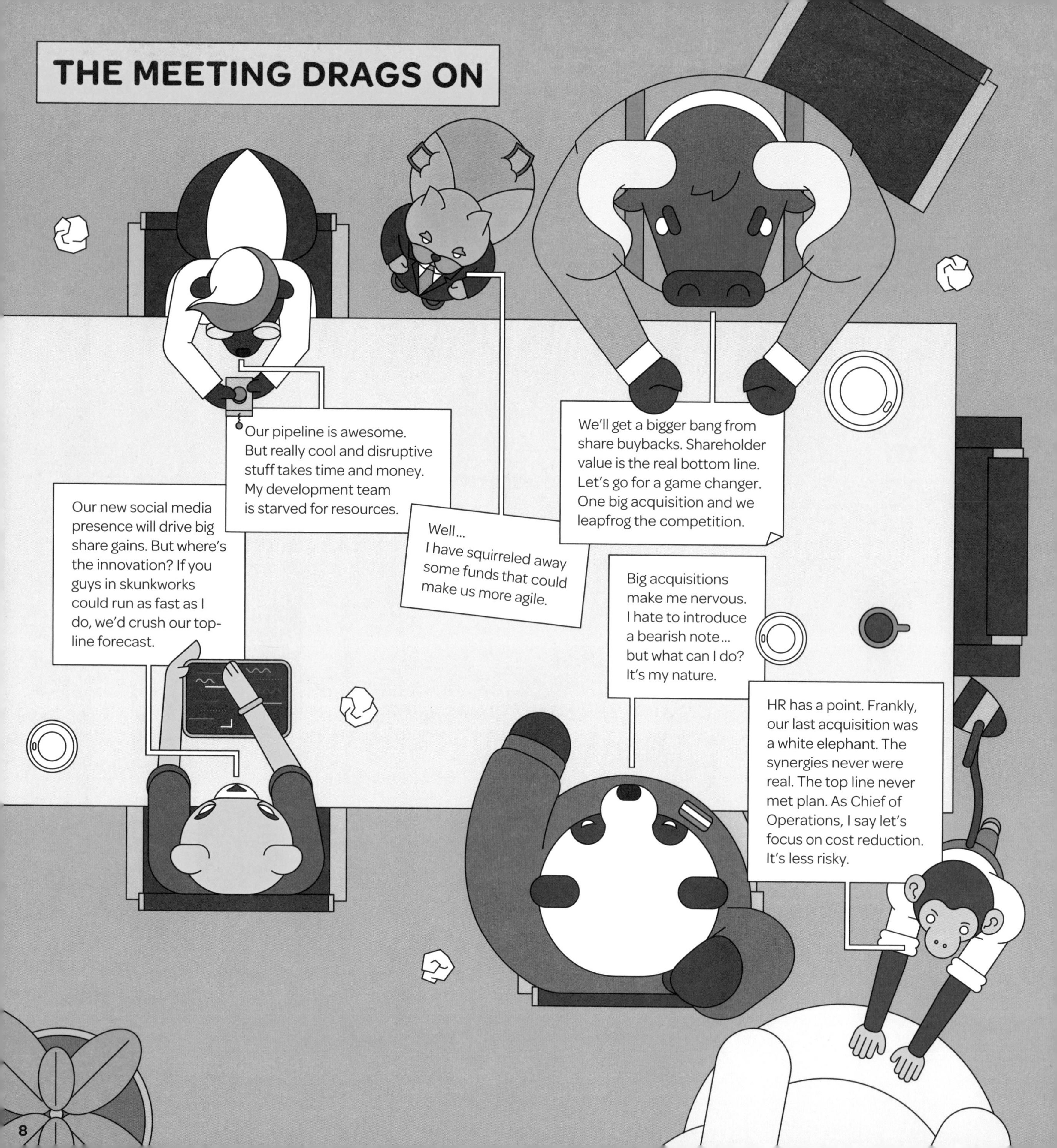

Our pipeline is awesome. But really cool and disruptive stuff takes time and money. My development team is starved for resources.
We'll get a bigger bang from share buybacks. Shareholder value is the real bottom line. Let's go for a game changer. One big acquisition and we leapfrog the competition.
Our new social media presence will drive big share gains. But where's the innovation? If you guys in skunkworks could run as fast as I do, we'd crush our top-line forecast.
Well... I have squirreled away some funds that could make us more agile.
Big acquisitions make me nervous. I hate to introduce a bearish note... but what can I do? It's my nature.
HR has a point. Frankly, our last acquisition was a white elephant. The synergies never were real. The top line never met plan. As Chief of Operations, I say let's focus on cost reduction. It's less risky.

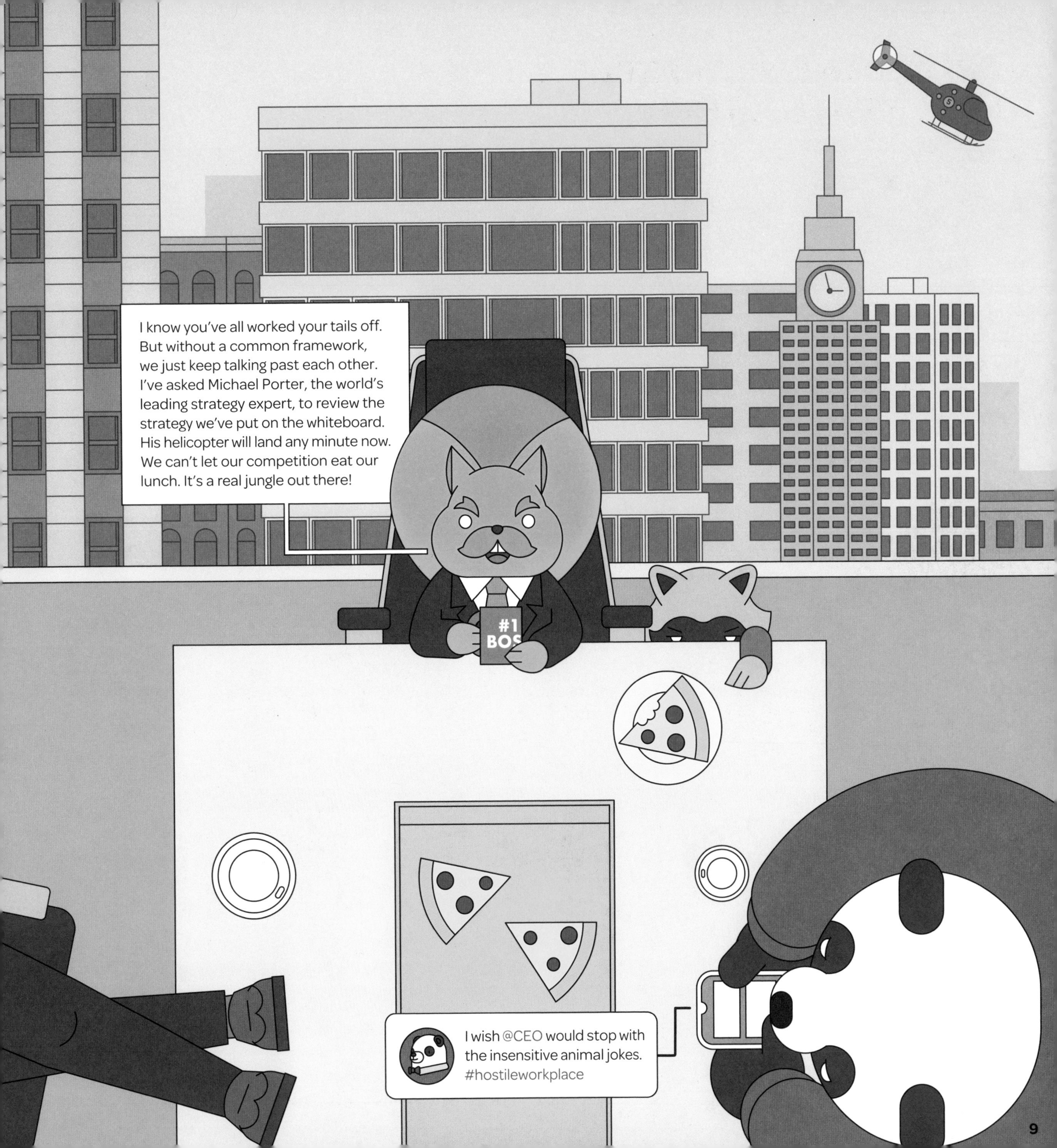
I know you've all worked your tails off. But without a common framework, we just keep talking past each other. I've asked Michael Porter, the world's leading strategy expert, to review the strategy we've put on the whiteboard. His helicopter will land any minute now. We can't let our competition eat our lunch. It's a real jungle out there!
#1 BOS
I wish @CEO would stop with the insensitive animal jokes. #hostileworkplace

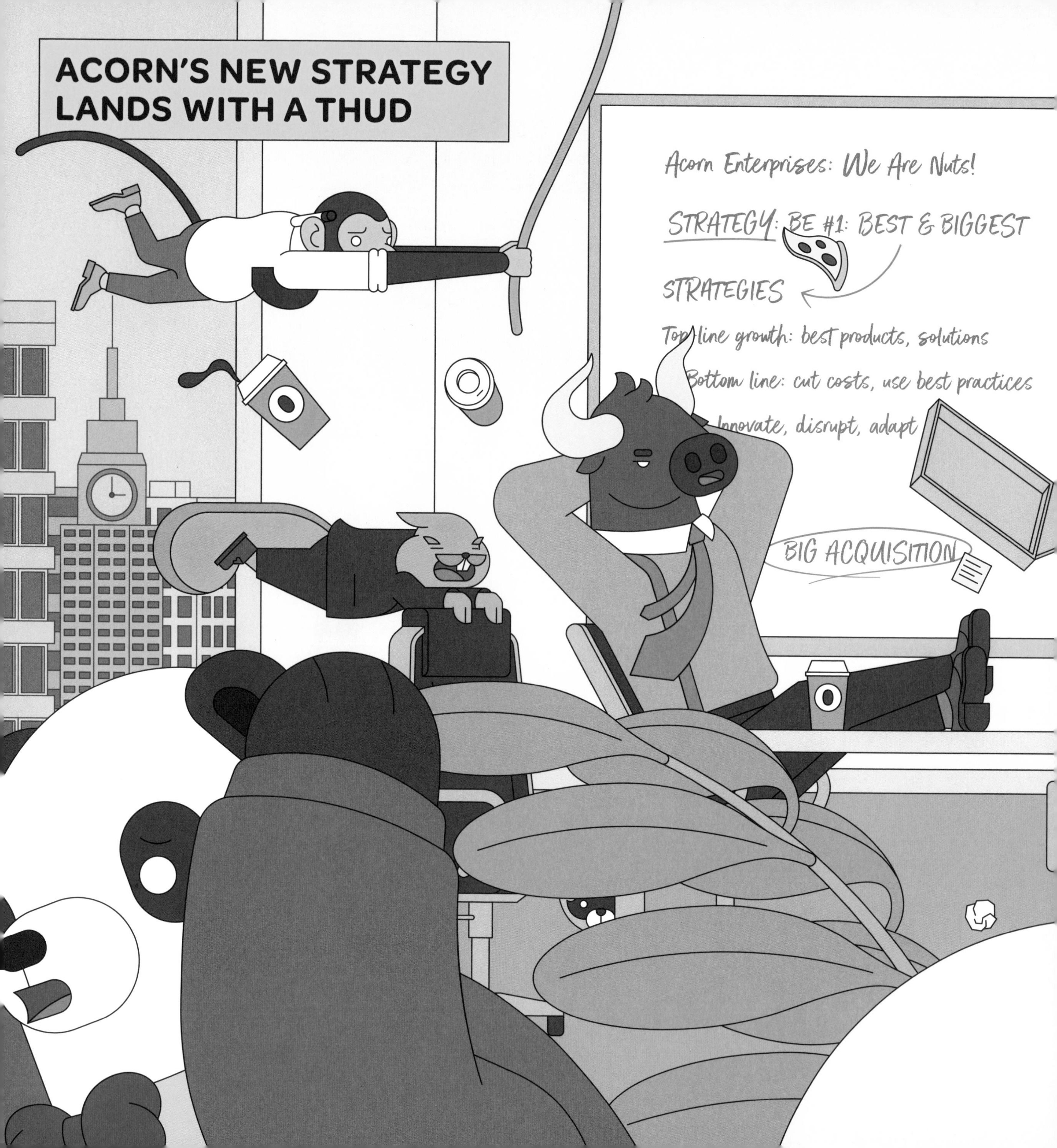
ACORN'S NEW STRATEGY LANDS WITH A THUD
Acorn Enterprises: We Are Nuts!
STRATEGY: BE #1: BEST & BIGGEST
STRATEGIES
Top line growth: best products, solutions
Bottom line: cut costs, use best practices
Innovate, disrupt, adapt
BIG ACQUISITION

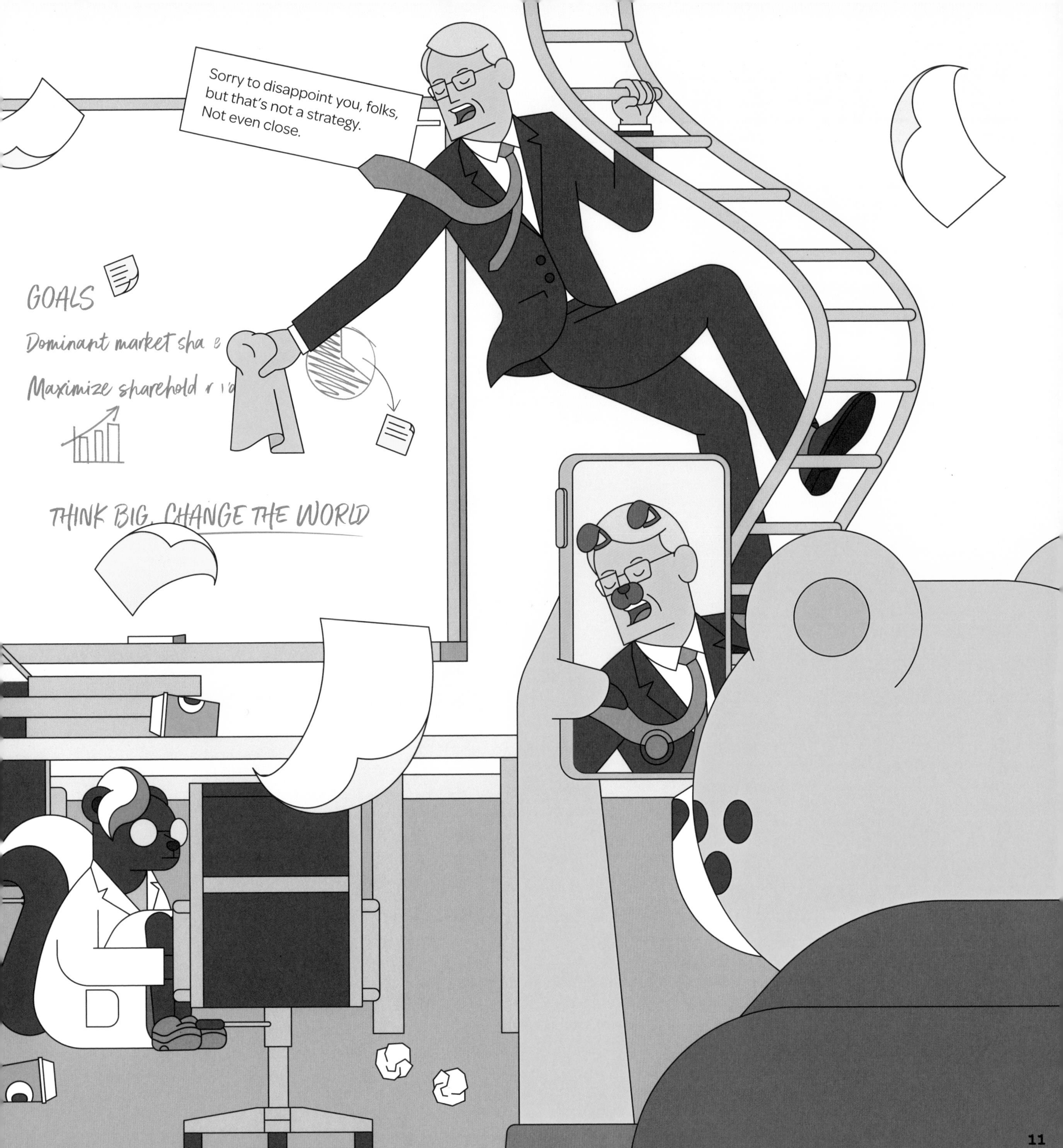
Sorry to disappoint you, folks, but that's not a strategy. Not even close.
GOALS
Dominant market sha e
Maximize sharehold r
THINK BIG, CHANGE THE WORLD

WHAT STRATEGY ISN'T

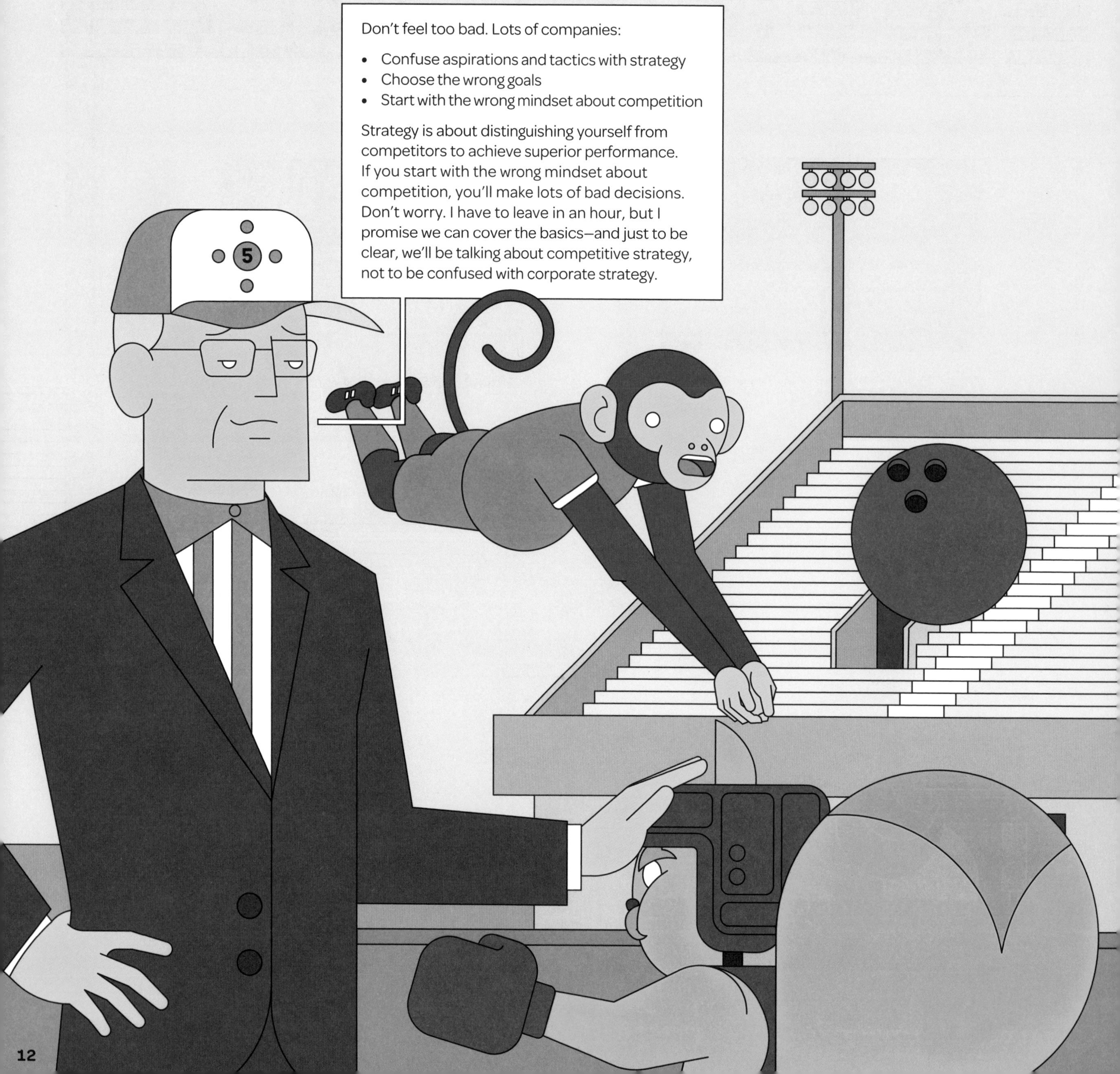
Don't feel too bad. Lots of companies:
• Confuse aspirations and tactics with strategy
• Choose the wrong goals
• Start with the wrong mindset about competition
Strategy is about distinguishing yourself from competitors to achieve superior performance. If you start with the wrong mindset about competition, you'll make lots of bad decisions. Don't worry. I have to leave in an hour, but I promise we can cover the basics—and just to be clear, we'll be talking about competitive strategy, not to be confused with corporate strategy.
5

STRATEGY

COMPETITIVE STRATEGY

Competitive strategy refers to the choices about how to compete in an individual business. That's the core level where competition takes place and where *competitive advantage* is won or lost. That's our focus today.

VS

CORPORATE STRATEGY

Corporate strategy is different. It refers to the overall strategy for a corporation that competes in multiple industries. The goal there is to assemble an attractive set of businesses and to integrate their strategies to enhance their collective *competitive advantage*.

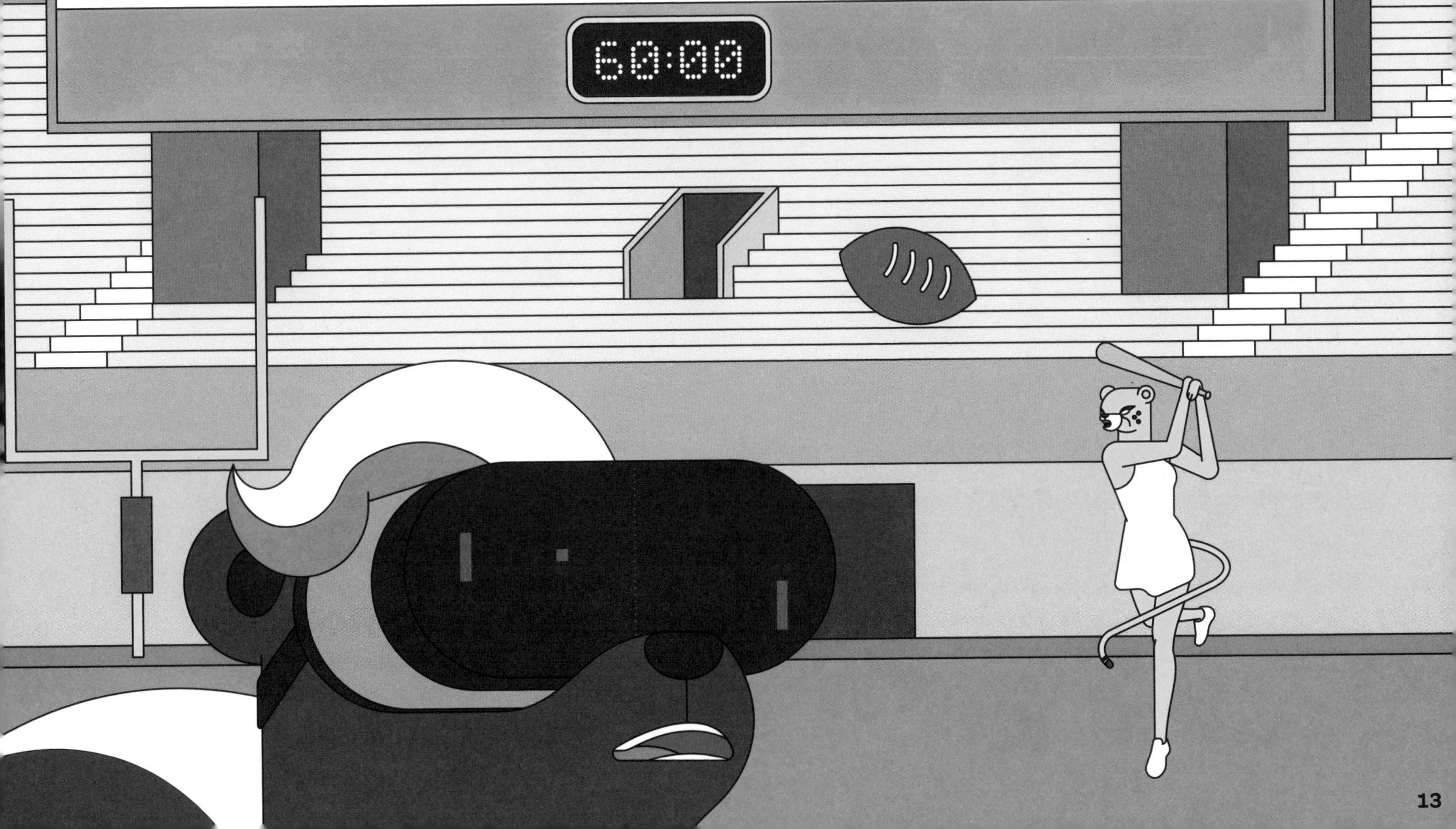
60:00

THE RIGHT MINDSET: BEST VS. UNIQUE

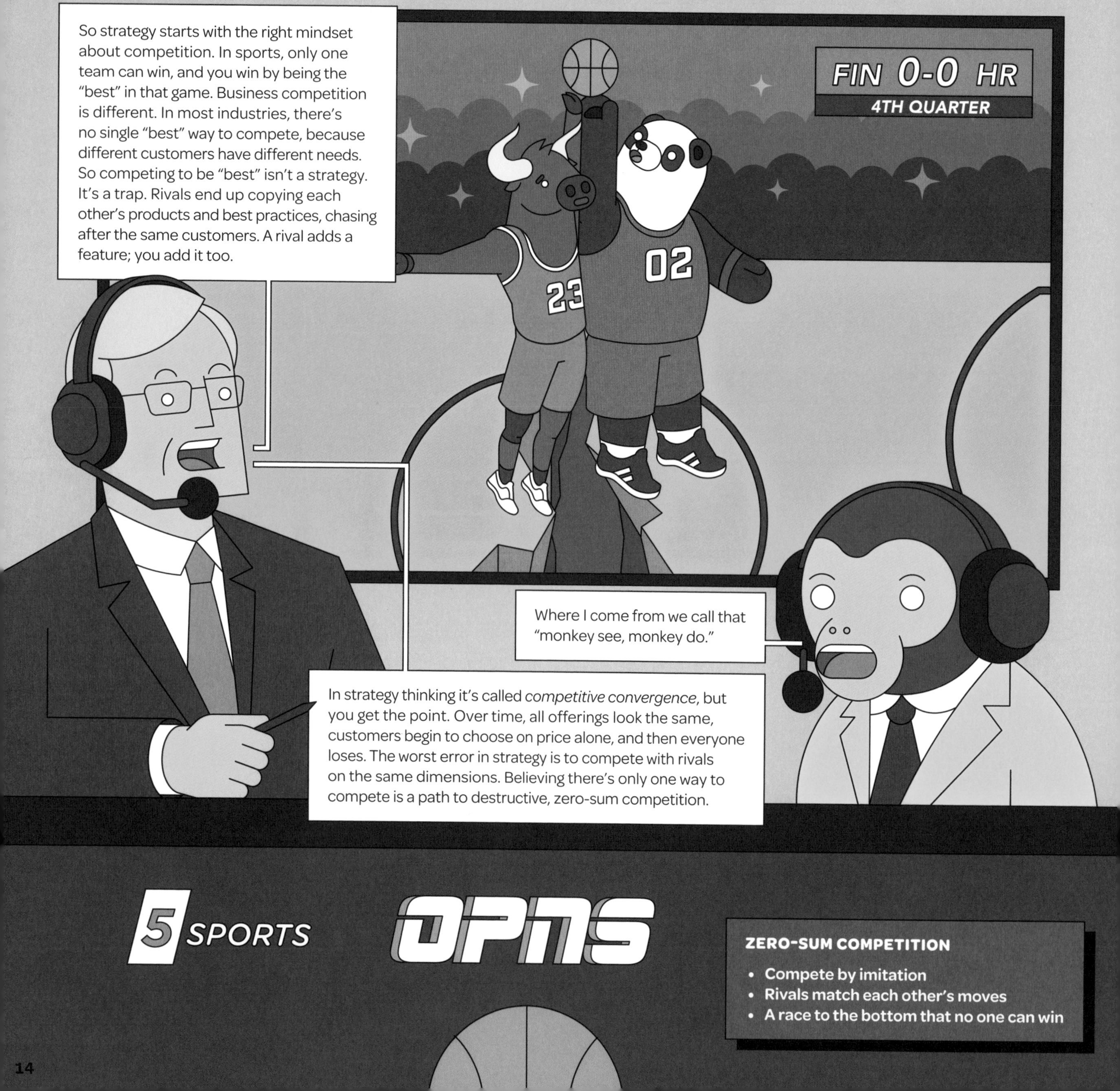
So strategy starts with the right mindset about competition. In sports, only one team can win, and you win by being the "best" in that game. Business competition is different. In most industries, there's no single "best" way to compete, because different customers have different needs. So competing to be "best" isn't a strategy. It's a trap. Rivals end up copying each other's products and best practices, chasing after the same customers. A rival adds a feature; you add it too.
FIN 0-0 HR
4TH QUARTER
23
02
Where I come from we call that "monkey see, monkey do."
In strategy thinking it's called *competitive convergence*, but you get the point. Over time, all offerings look the same, customers begin to choose on price alone, and then everyone loses. The worst error in strategy is to compete with rivals on the same dimensions. Believing there's only one way to compete is a path to destructive, zero-sum competition.
5 SPORTS
OPNS
ZERO-SUM COMPETITION
• Compete by imitation
• Rivals match each other's moves
• A race to the bottom that no one can win

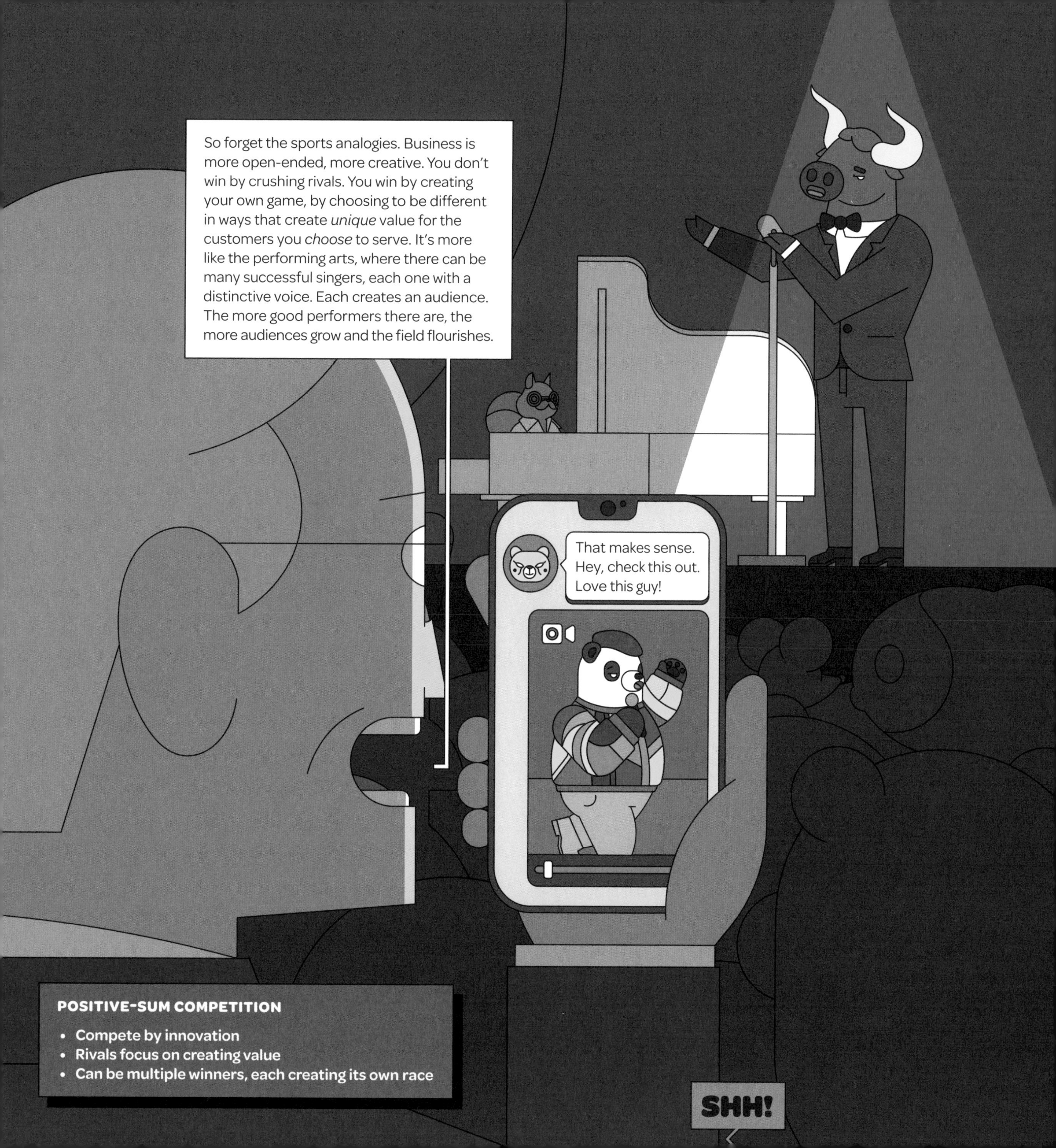

So forget the sports analogies. Business is more open-ended, more creative. You don't win by crushing rivals. You win by creating your own game, by choosing to be different in ways that create *unique* value for the customers you *choose* to serve. It's more like the performing arts, where there can be many successful singers, each one with a distinctive voice. Each creates an audience. The more good performers there are, the more audiences grow and the field flourishes.
That makes sense. Hey, check this out. Love this guy!
POSITIVE-SUM COMPETITION
• Compete by innovation
• Rivals focus on creating value
• Can be multiple winners, each creating its own race
SHH!

THE RIGHT GOAL: PROFITABILITY, NOT SIZE

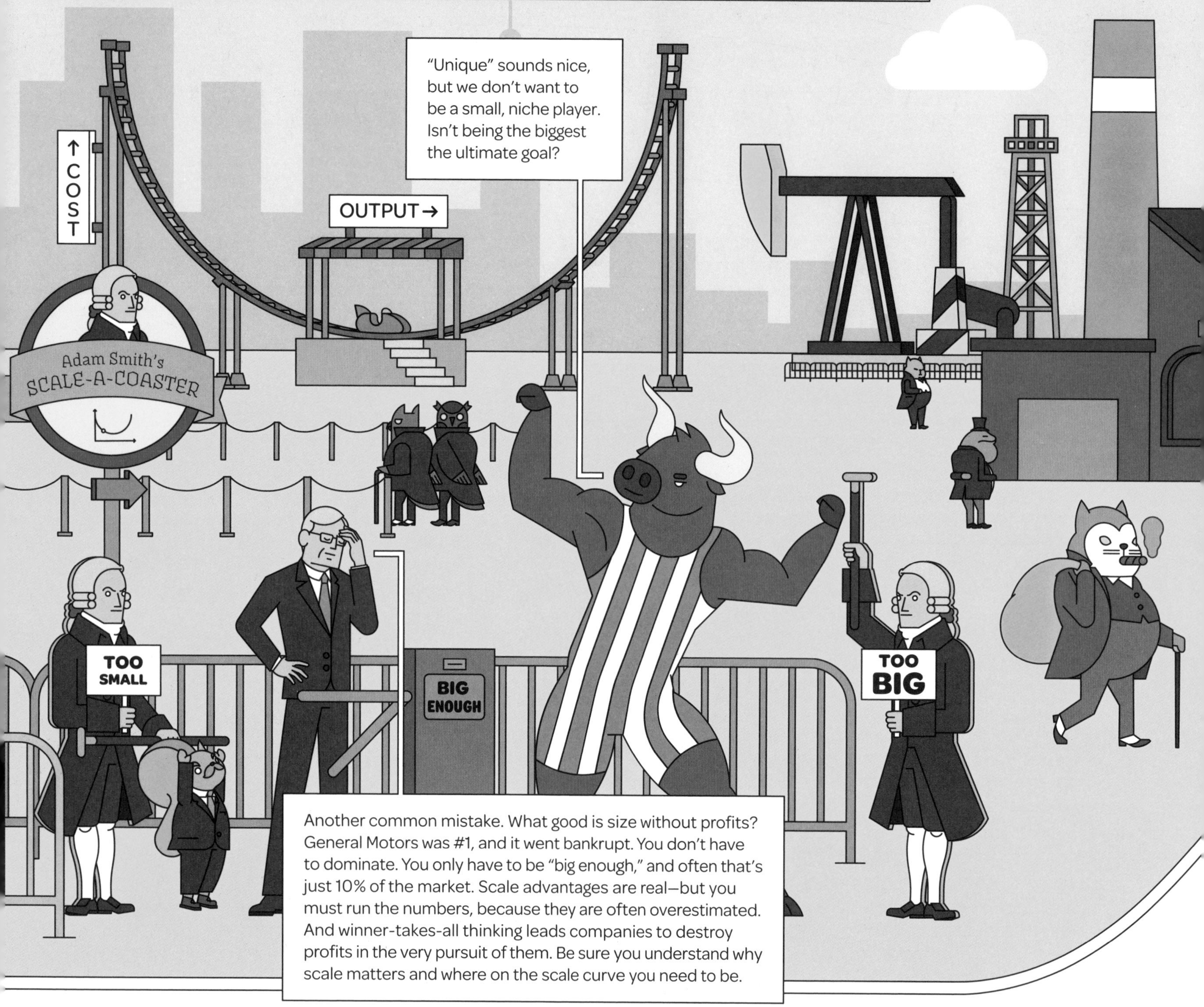
"Unique" sounds nice, but we don't want to be a small, niche player. Isn't being the biggest the ultimate goal?
↑ COST
OUTPUT →
Adam Smith's SCALE-A-COASTER
TOO SMALL
BIG ENOUGH
TOO BIG
Another common mistake. What good is size without profits? General Motors was #1, and it went bankrupt. You don't have to dominate. You only have to be "big enough," and often that's just 10% of the market. Scale advantages are real—but you must run the numbers, because they are often overestimated. And winner-takes-all thinking leads companies to destroy profits in the very pursuit of them. Be sure you understand why scale matters and where on the scale curve you need to be.

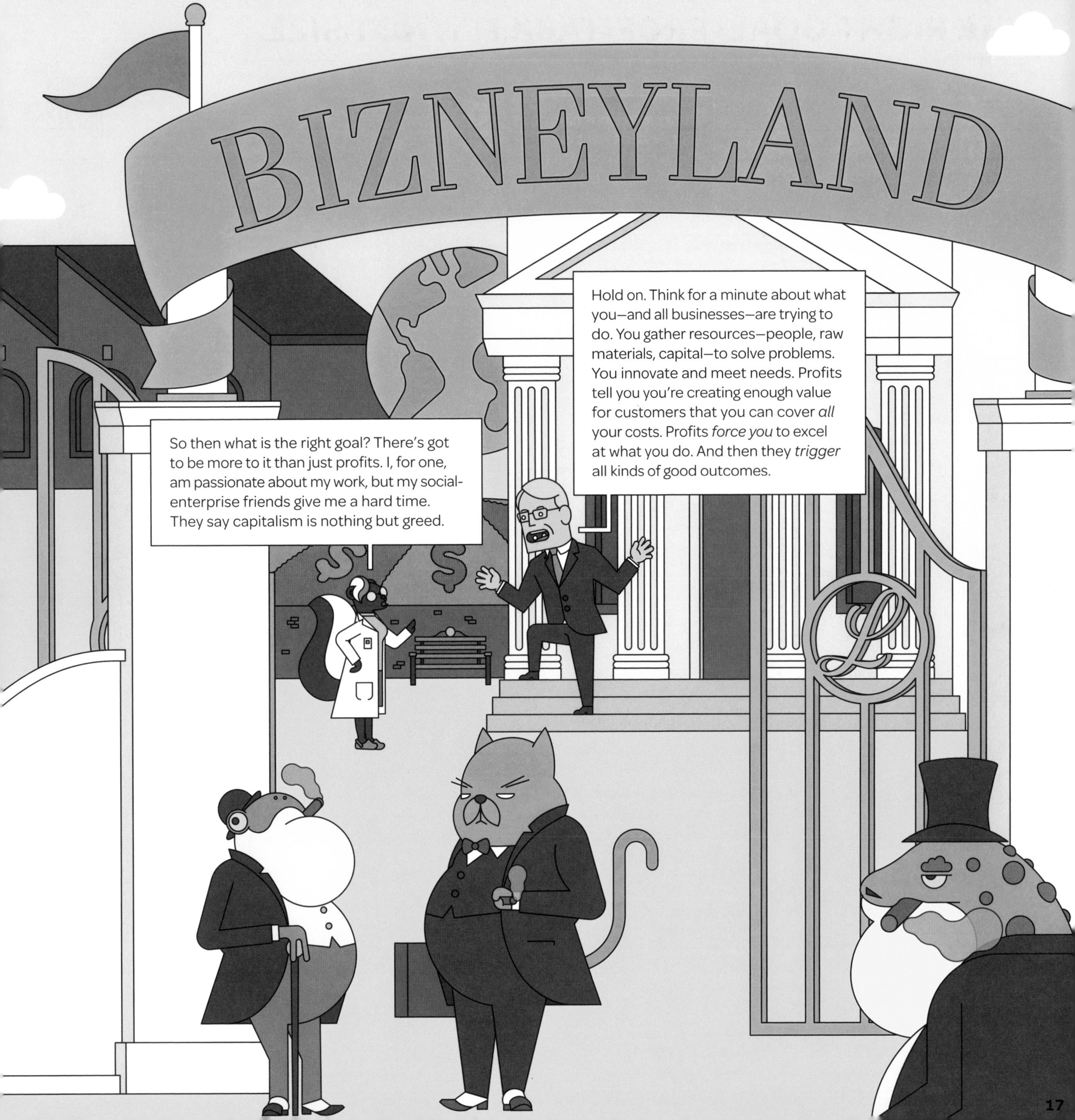
BIZNEYLAND
So then what is the right goal? There's got to be more to it than just profits. I, for one, am passionate about my work, but my social-enterprise friends give me a hard time. They say capitalism is nothing but greed.
Hold on. Think for a minute about what you—and all businesses—are trying to do. You gather resources—people, raw materials, capital—to solve problems. You innovate and meet needs. Profits tell you you're creating enough value for customers that you can cover *all* your costs. Profits *force you* to excel at what you do. And then they *trigger* all kinds of good outcomes.

THE RIGHT GOAL: PROFITS AND SOCIETY

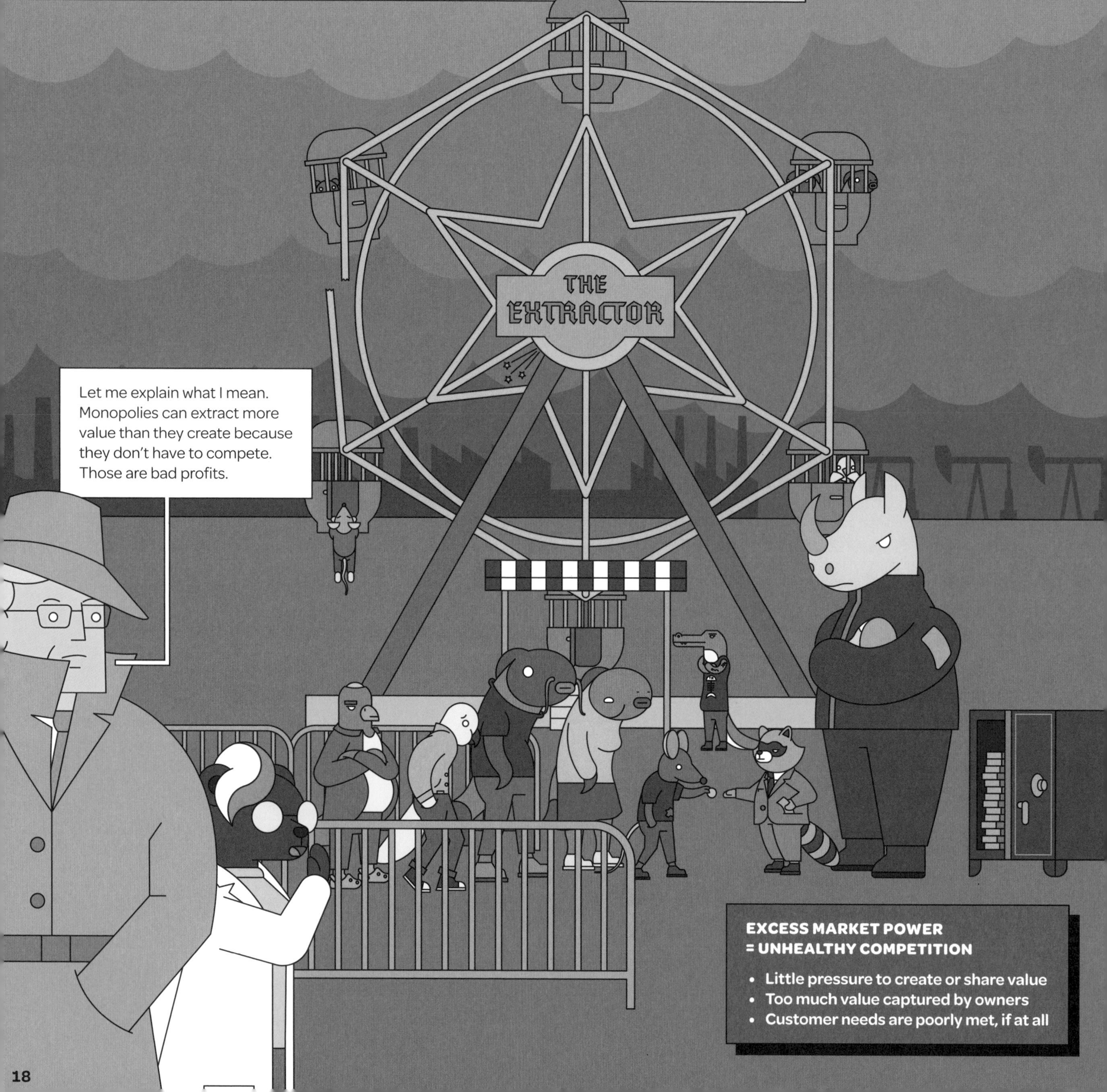

Let me explain what I mean. Monopolies can extract more value than they create because they don't have to compete. Those are bad profits.
THE EXTRACTOR
EXCESS MARKET POWER
= UNHEALTHY COMPETITION
• Little pressure to create or share value
• Too much value captured by owners
• Customer needs are poorly met, if at all

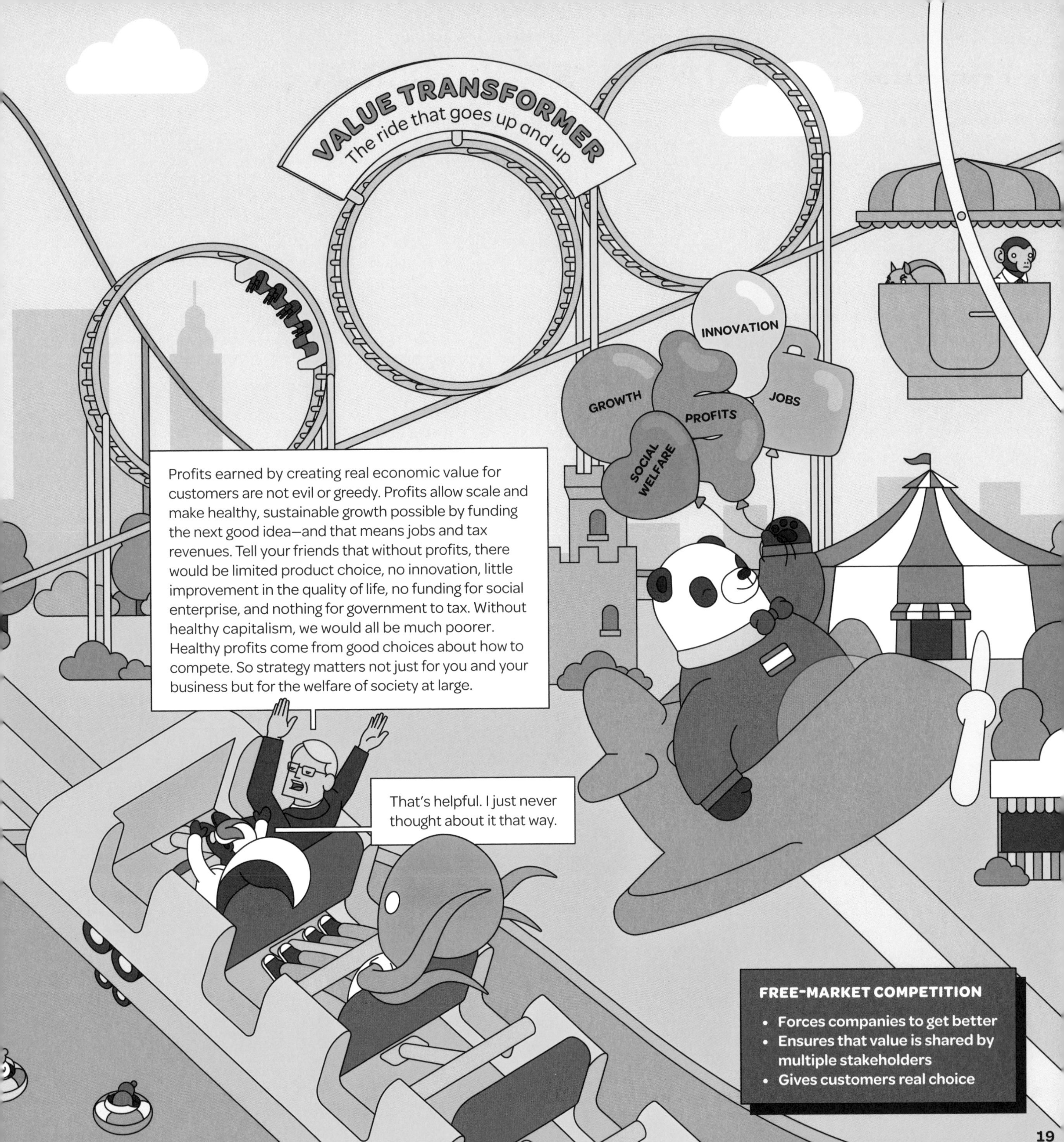
VALUE TRANSFORMER
The ride that goes up and up
INNOVATION
GROWTH
PROFITS
JOBS
SOCIAL WELFARE
Profits earned by creating real economic value for customers are not evil or greedy. Profits allow scale and make healthy, sustainable growth possible by funding the next good idea—and that means jobs and tax revenues. Tell your friends that without profits, there would be limited product choice, no innovation, little improvement in the quality of life, no funding for social enterprise, and nothing for government to tax. Without healthy capitalism, we would all be much poorer. Healthy profits come from good choices about how to compete. So strategy matters not just for you and your business but for the welfare of society at large.
That's helpful. I just never thought about it that way.
FREE-MARKET COMPETITION
• Forces companies to get better
• Ensures that value is shared by multiple stakeholders
• Gives customers real choice

THE RIGHT GOAL: MAKING GOOD USE OF CAPITAL

Your job is to make good use of the capital you need to run the business. Return on invested capital (ROIC) weighs the profits a business generates against the capital invested in it. Superior ROIC—sustainable over years, not just in the next quarter—tells you you're creating value *and* making good use of capital. Unfortunately, short-term shareholder value drives a lot of executive behavior, but it is a spectacularly unreliable goal. Pleasing current shareholders is *not* the goal of strategy. Stock price is a meaningful measure of economic value only over the long run. So be careful about the goals you choose—very careful.

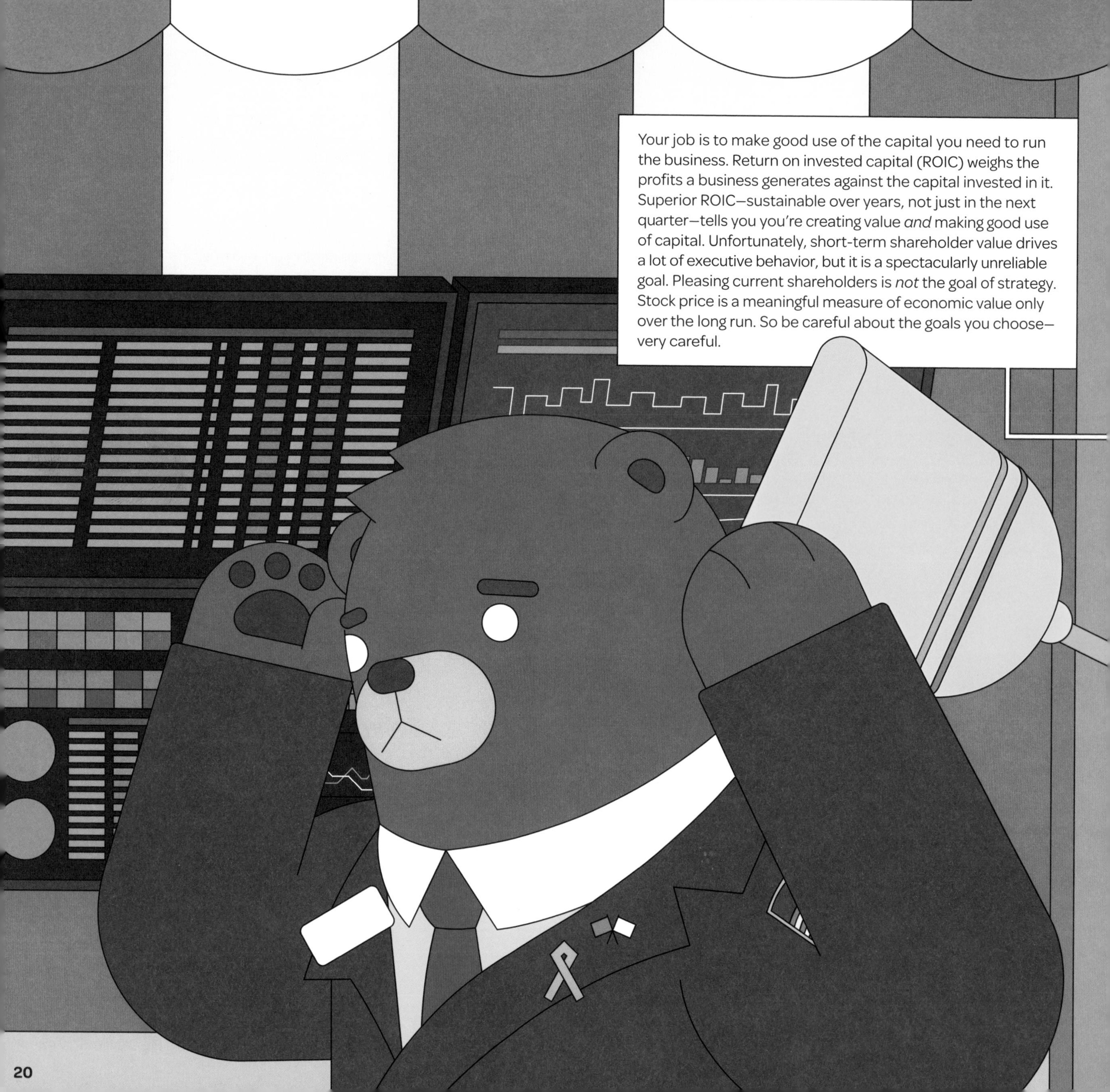

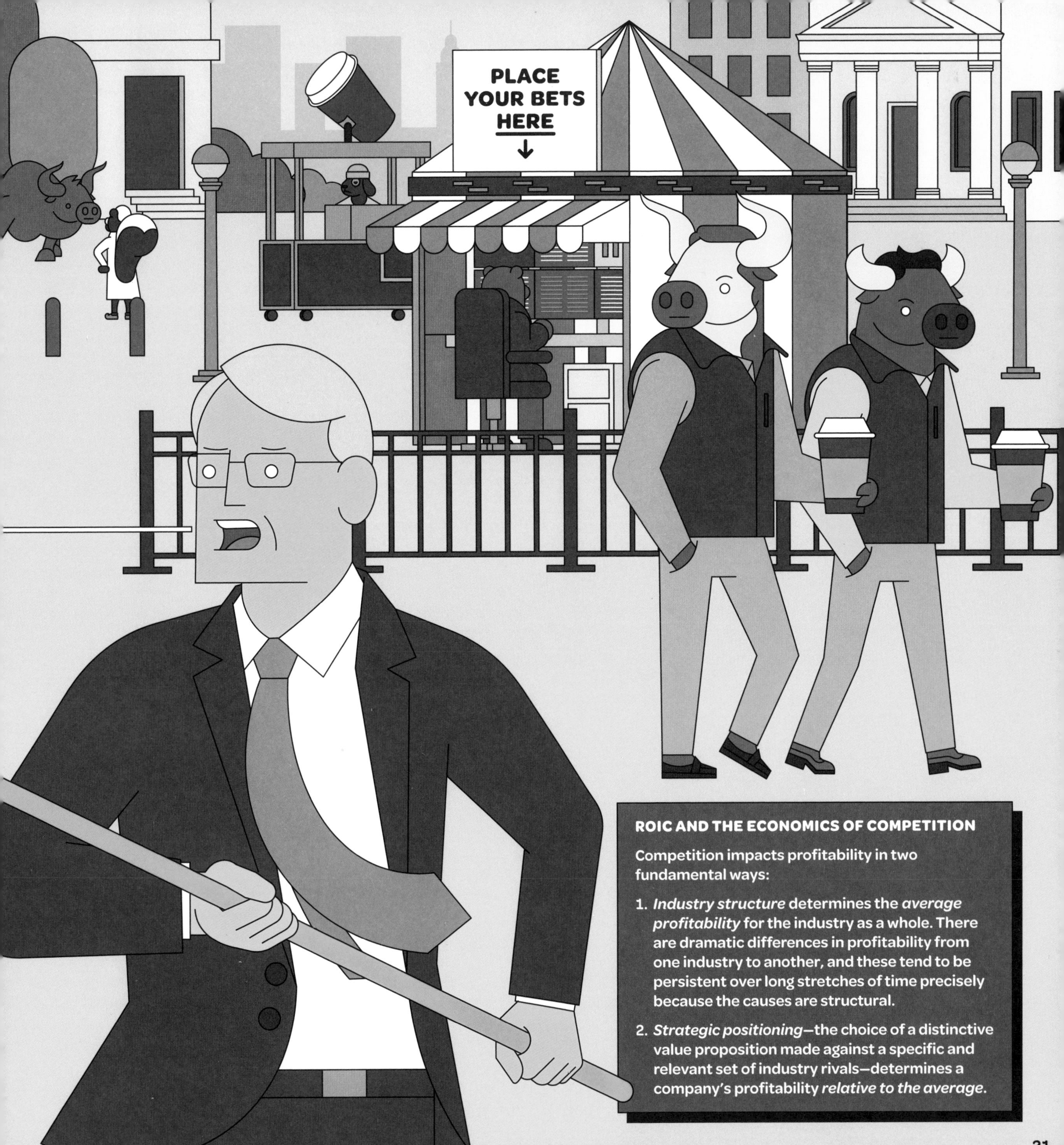
PLACE
YOUR BETS
HERE

ROIC AND THE ECONOMICS OF COMPETITION

Competition impacts profitability in two fundamental ways:

1. *Industry structure* determines the *average profitability* for the industry as a whole. There are dramatic differences in profitability from one industry to another, and these tend to be persistent over long stretches of time precisely because the causes are structural.
2. *Strategic positioning*—the choice of a distinctive value proposition made against a specific and relevant set of industry rivals—determines a company's profitability *relative to the average*.

COMPETITION AND INDUSTRY STRUCTURE

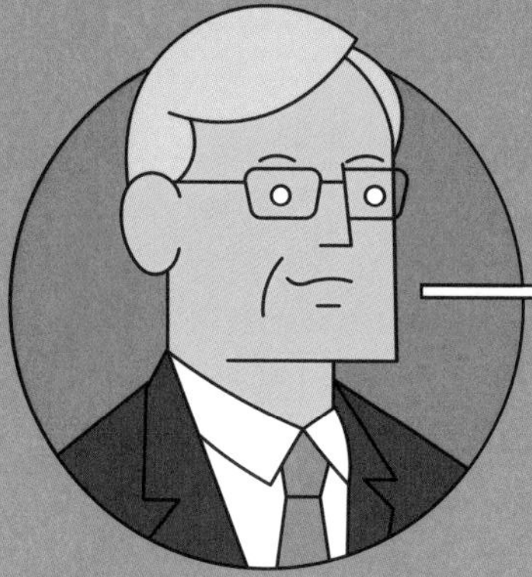

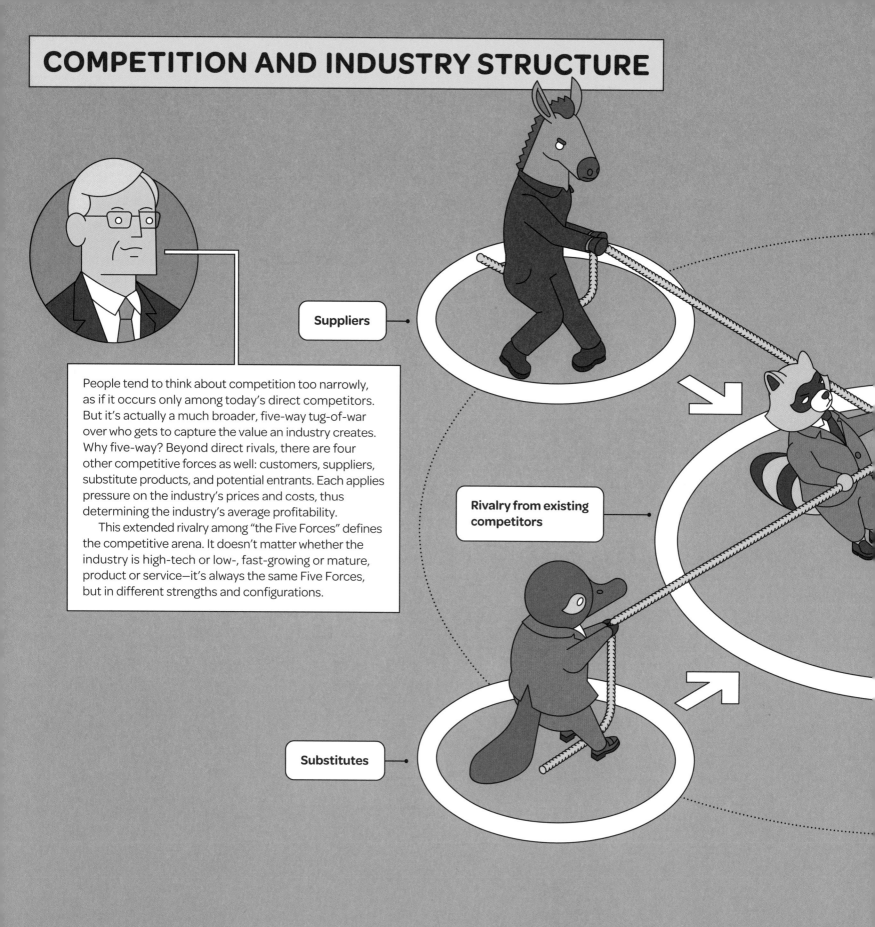

People tend to think about competition too narrowly, as if it occurs only among today's direct competitors. But it's actually a much broader, five-way tug-of-war over who gets to capture the value an industry creates. Why five-way? Beyond direct rivals, there are four other competitive forces as well: customers, suppliers, substitute products, and potential entrants. Each applies pressure on the industry's prices and costs, thus determining the industry's average profitability.

This extended rivalry among "the Five Forces" defines the competitive arena. It doesn't matter whether the industry is high-tech or low-, fast-growing or mature, product or service—it's always the same Five Forces, but in different strengths and configurations.

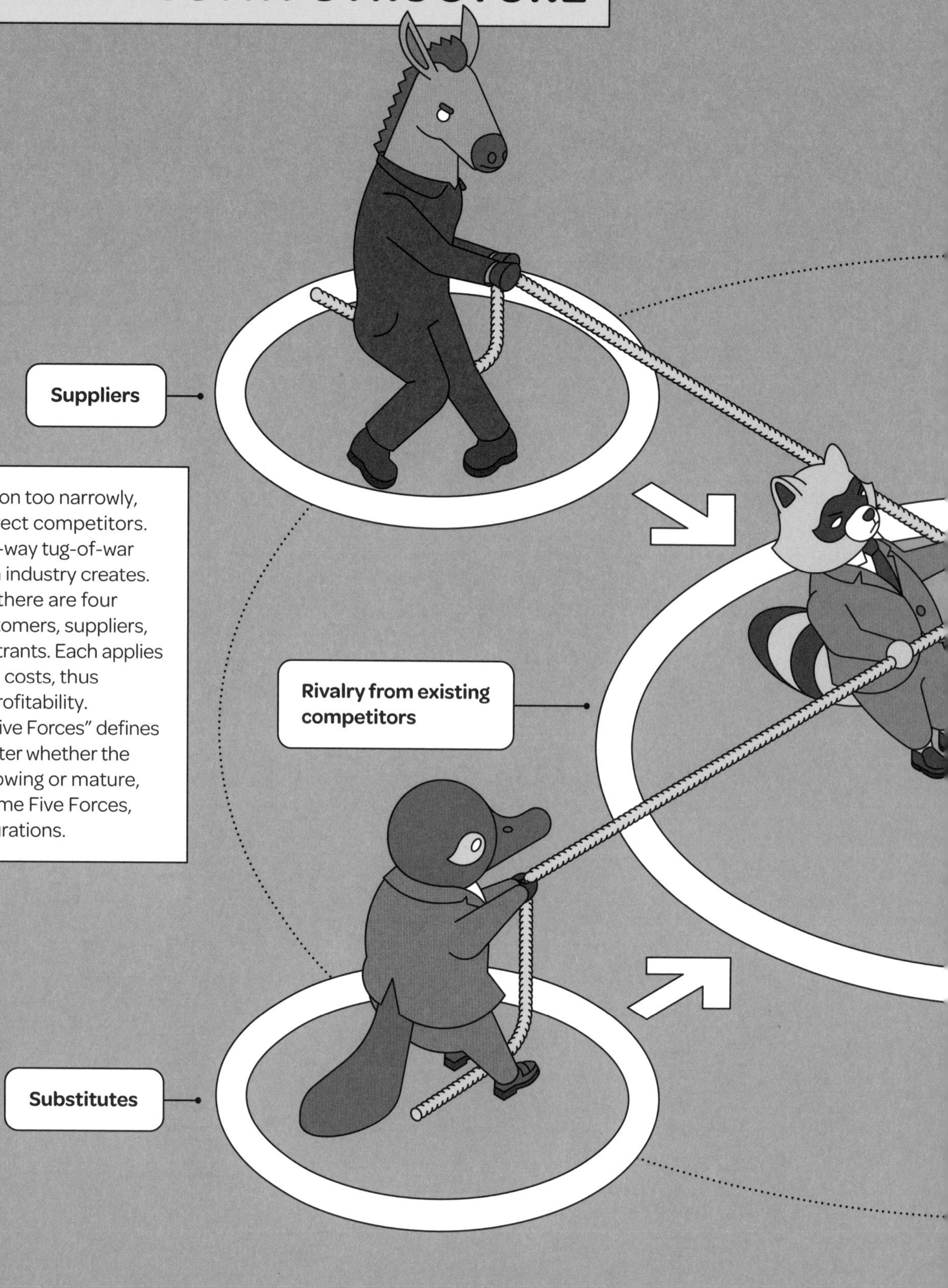
Suppliers
Rivalry from existing competitors
Substitutes

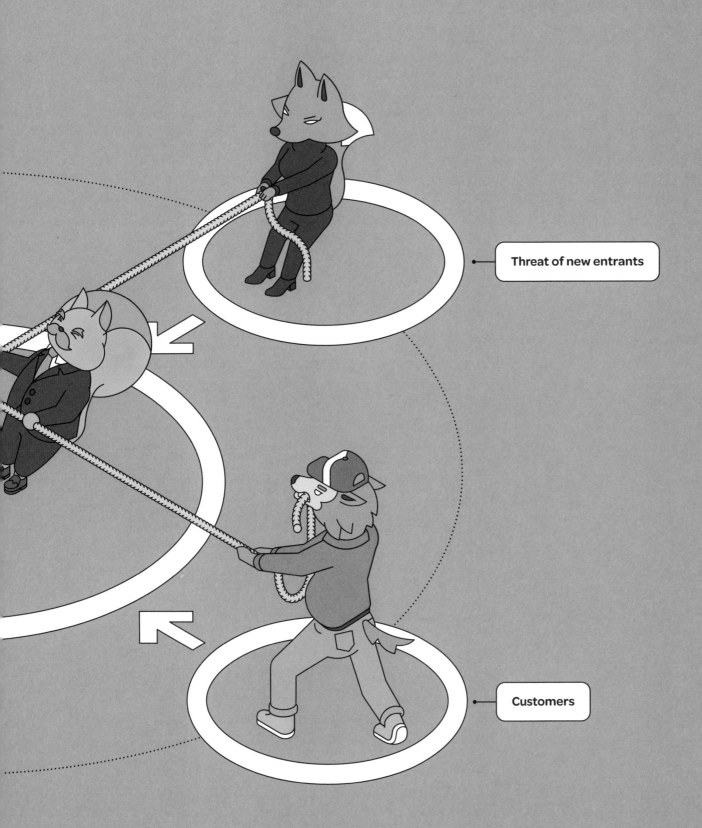

Threat of new entrants

Customers

THE FIVE FORCES DRIVE EVERY INDUSTRY'S PROFITABILITY

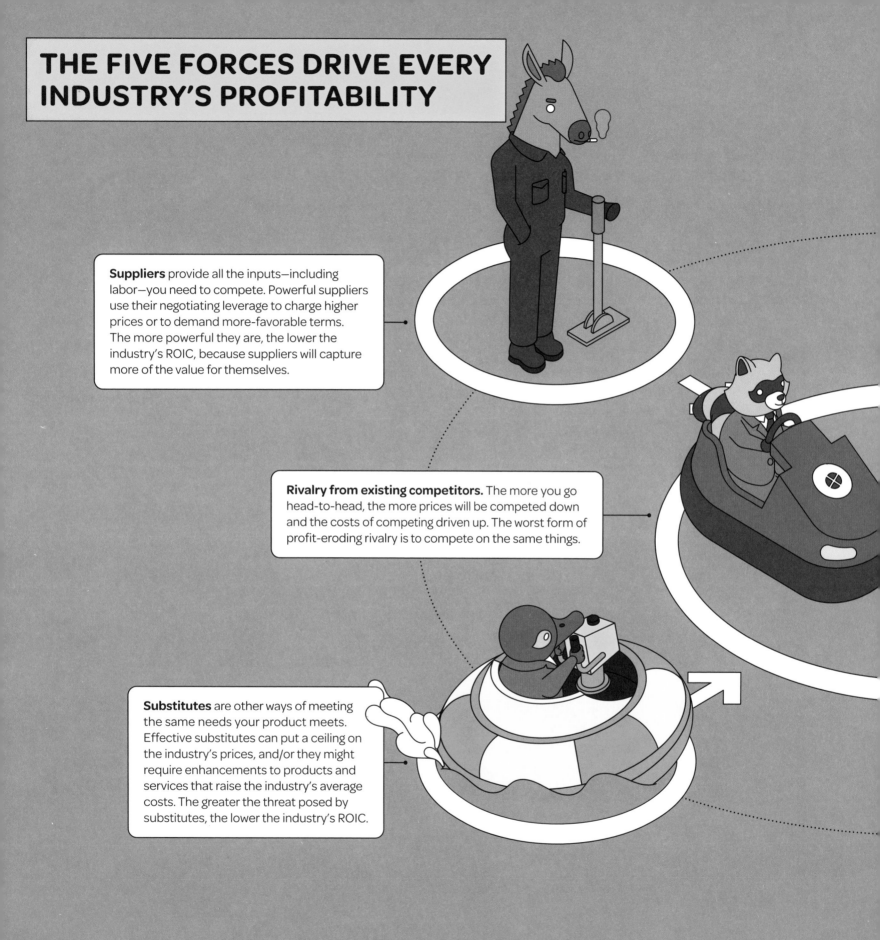

Suppliers provide all the inputs—including labor—you need to compete. Powerful suppliers use their negotiating leverage to charge higher prices or to demand more-favorable terms. The more powerful they are, the lower the industry's ROIC, because suppliers will capture more of the value for themselves.

Rivalry from existing competitors. The more you go head-to-head, the more prices will be competed down and the costs of competing driven up. The worst form of profit-eroding rivalry is to compete on the same things.

Substitutes are other ways of meeting the same needs your product meets. Effective substitutes can put a ceiling on the industry's prices, and/or they might require enhancements to products and services that raise the industry's average costs. The greater the threat posed by substitutes, the lower the industry's ROIC.

Threat of new entrants. Entry barriers protect an industry from new competitors and enable high profitability. How high are the hurdles a new entrant would have to jump over? What scale is required to be competitive? Are entrenched brands a barrier? High entry barriers give companies greater freedom to raise prices. Low barriers put a limit on prices and profits.

Customers refers to end users and, where relevant, the channels used to reach them. When customers put pressure on prices, or demand more features but won't pay more for them, they are competing with you over profits. Some customer segments have more or less negotiating power and price sensitivity. The more bargaining power customers and channels have, the less profitable the industry will be.

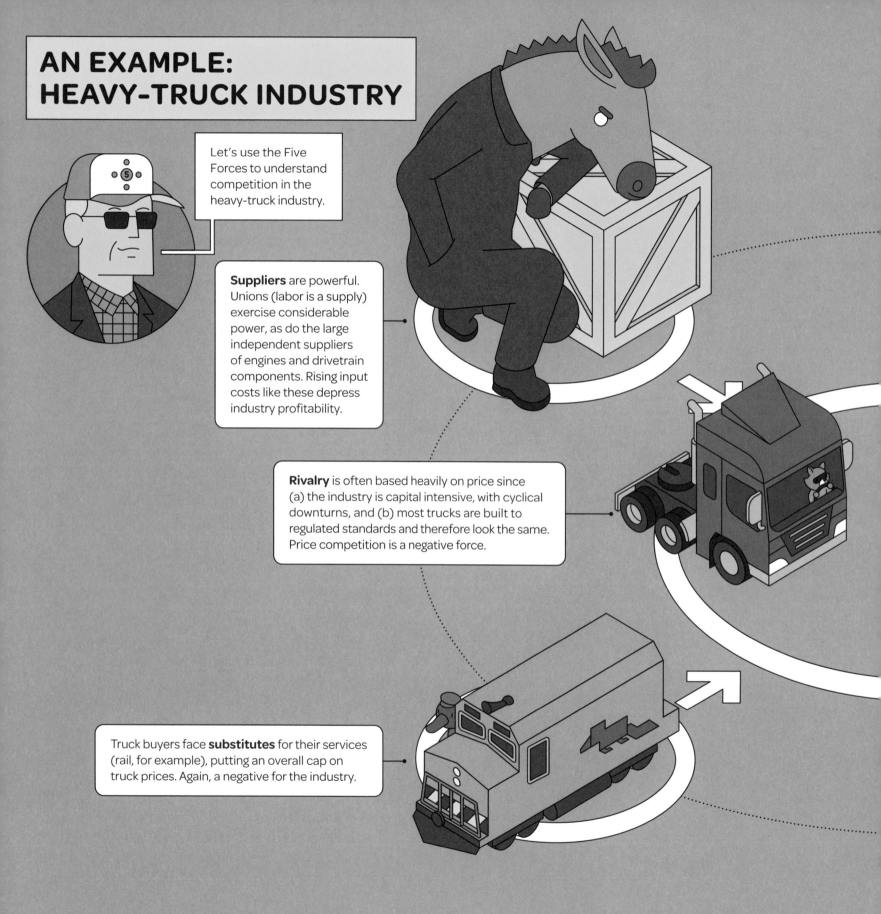

AN EXAMPLE: HEAVY-TRUCK INDUSTRY

Let's use the Five Forces to understand competition in the heavy-truck industry.

Suppliers are powerful. Unions (labor is a supply) exercise considerable power, as do the large independent suppliers of engines and drivetrain components. Rising input costs like these depress industry profitability.

Rivalry is often based heavily on price since (a) the industry is capital intensive, with cyclical downturns, and (b) most trucks are built to regulated standards and therefore look the same. Price competition is a negative force.

Truck buyers face **substitutes** for their services (rail, for example), putting an overall cap on truck prices. Again, a negative for the industry.

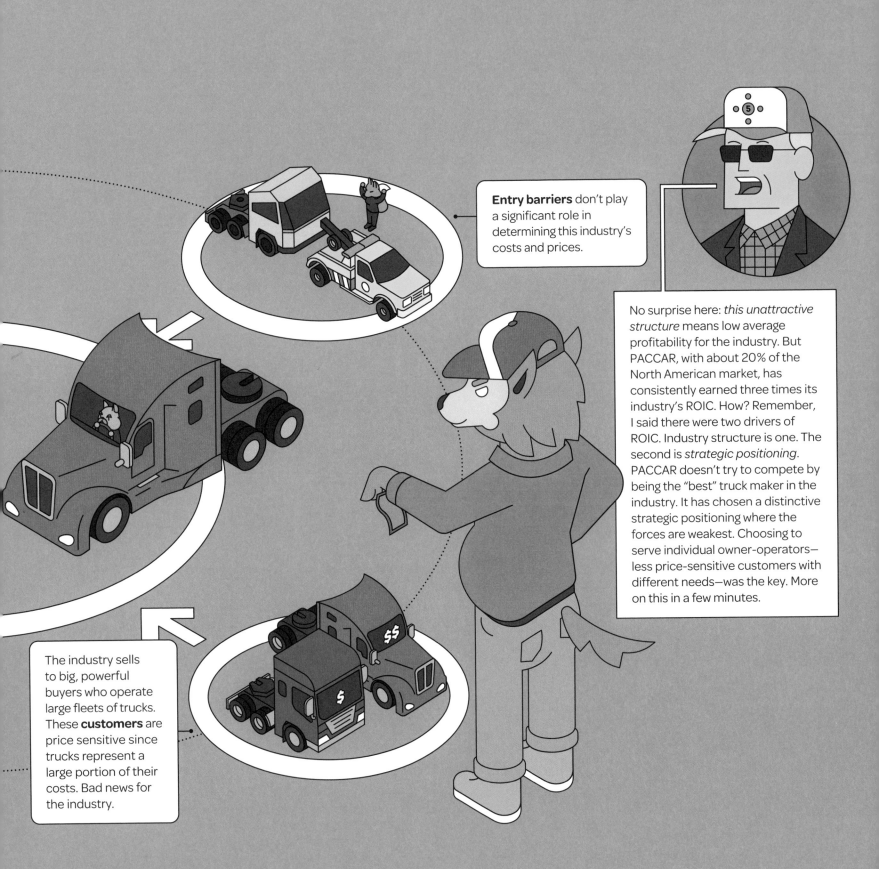

Entry barriers don't play a significant role in determining this industry's costs and prices.

No surprise here: *this unattractive structure* means low average profitability for the industry. But PACCAR, with about 20% of the North American market, has consistently earned three times its industry's ROIC. How? Remember, I said there were two drivers of ROIC. Industry structure is one. The second is *strategic positioning*. PACCAR doesn't try to compete by being the "best" truck maker in the industry. It has chosen a distinctive strategic positioning where the forces are weakest. Choosing to serve individual owner-operators—less price-sensitive customers with different needs—was the key. More on this in a few minutes.

The industry sells to big, powerful buyers who operate large fleets of trucks. These **customers** are price sensitive since trucks represent a large portion of their costs. Bad news for the industry.

DEFINING YOUR INDUSTRY

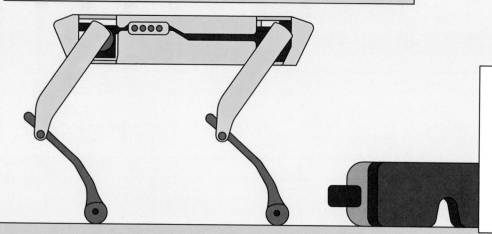

That is actually a very good question. Defining your industry properly is critical. Many companies fail precisely because they get this wrong. Tech is too broad; so is manufacturing or entertainment. And if a railroad defines itself as a transportation company, what's next? Acquire an airline? As dumb as it sounds, strategy disasters like that are common when you get the industry definition wrong. Business definition also includes assessing whether the geographic scope is local, regional, national, or global.

Can I ask a stupid question? What exactly is an industry? Is tech an industry? Do all tech companies really compete with each other? Is railroad itself an industry, or is it in the transportation industry?

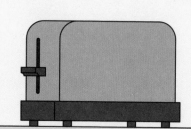

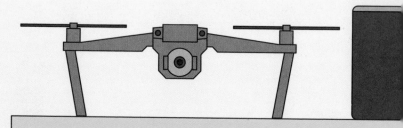

WHAT IS AN INDUSTRY?

Think about an industry as a group of players who share the same basic set of Five Forces. Are you facing the same buyers, the same suppliers, the same entry barriers, and so forth? Where there are differences in more than one force, or where differences in any one force are large, you are likely dealing with distinct industries. Each one will need its own strategy. For geographic scope, ask whether needs are similar across geographies. And, can your existing operating model be extended to new markets?

COMPETITION AND INDUSTRY STRUCTURE

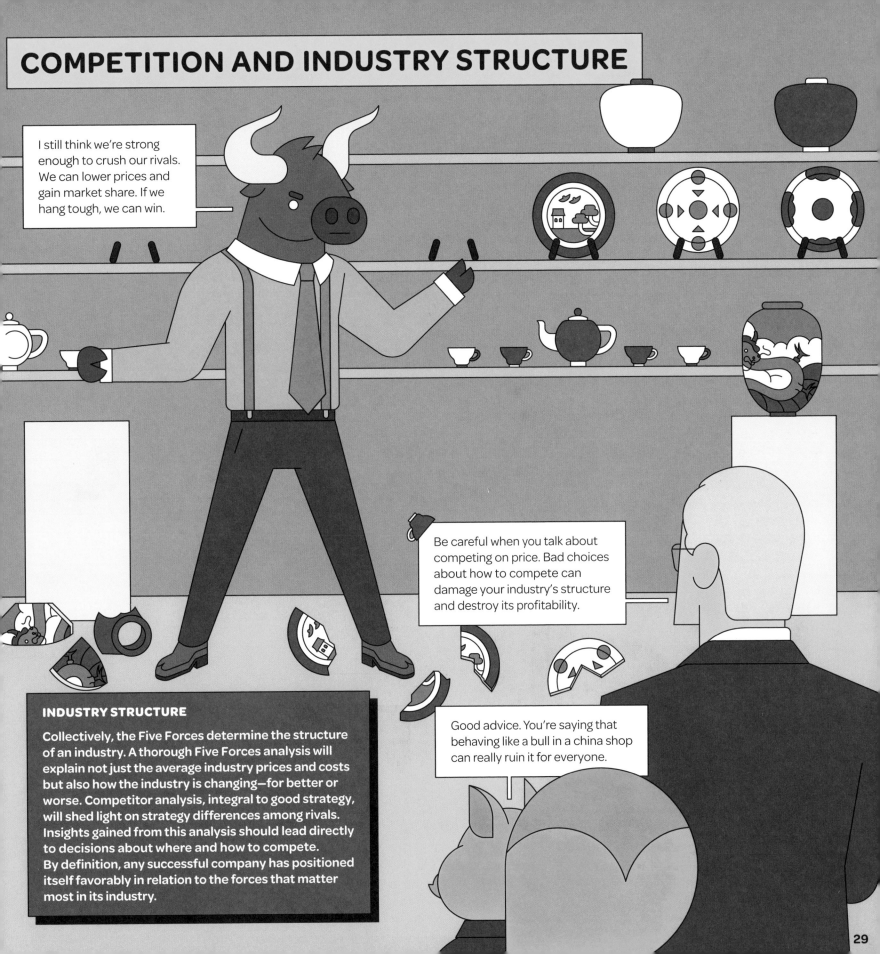

I still think we're strong enough to crush our rivals. We can lower prices and gain market share. If we hang tough, we can win.

Be careful when you talk about competing on price. Bad choices about how to compete can damage your industry's structure and destroy its profitability.

INDUSTRY STRUCTURE

Collectively, the Five Forces determine the structure of an industry. A thorough Five Forces analysis will explain not just the average industry prices and costs but also how the industry is changing—for better or worse. Competitor analysis, integral to good strategy, will shed light on strategy differences among rivals. Insights gained from this analysis should lead directly to decisions about where and how to compete. By definition, any successful company has positioned itself favorably in relation to the forces that matter most in its industry.

Good advice. You're saying that behaving like a bull in a china shop can really ruin it for everyone.

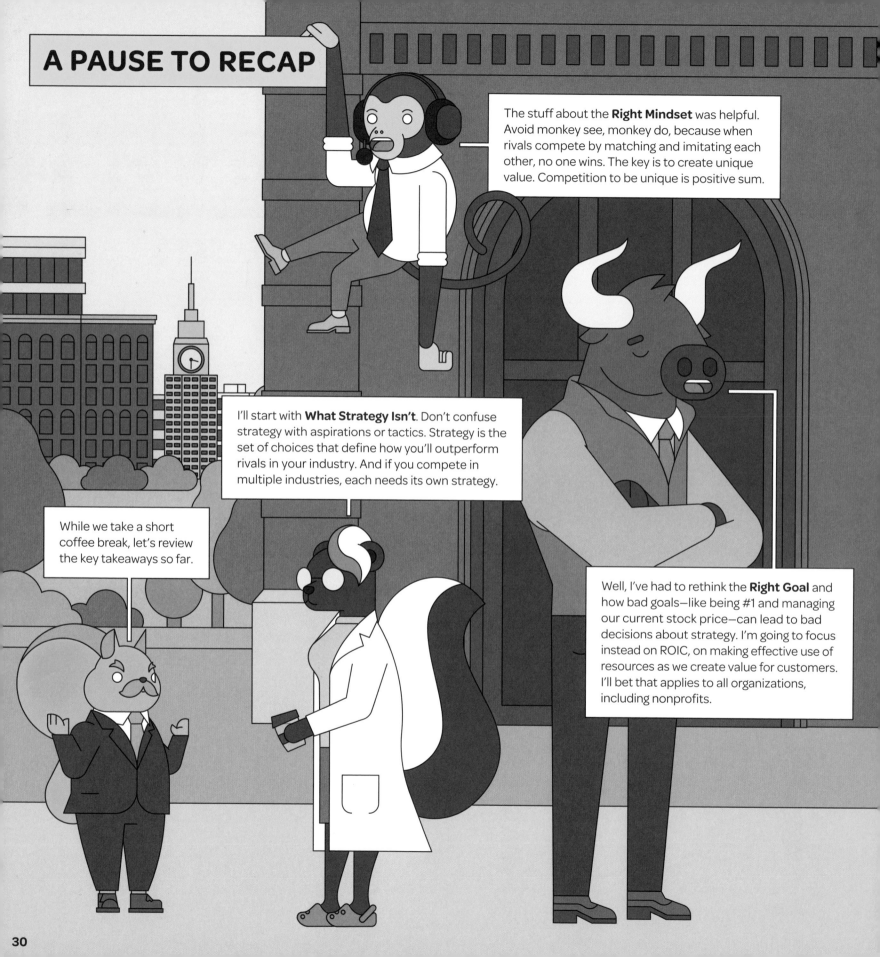

The stuff about the **Right Mindset** was helpful. Avoid monkey see, monkey do, because when rivals compete by matching and imitating each other, no one wins. The key is to create unique value. Competition to be unique is positive sum.

I'll start with **What Strategy Isn't**. Don't confuse strategy with aspirations or tactics. Strategy is the set of choices that define how you'll outperform rivals in your industry. And if you compete in multiple industries, each needs its own strategy.

While we take a short coffee break, let's review the key takeaways so far.

Well, I've had to rethink the **Right Goal** and how bad goals—like being #1 and managing our current stock price—can lead to bad decisions about strategy. I'm going to focus instead on ROIC, on making effective use of resources as we create value for customers. I'll bet that applies to all organizations, including nonprofits.

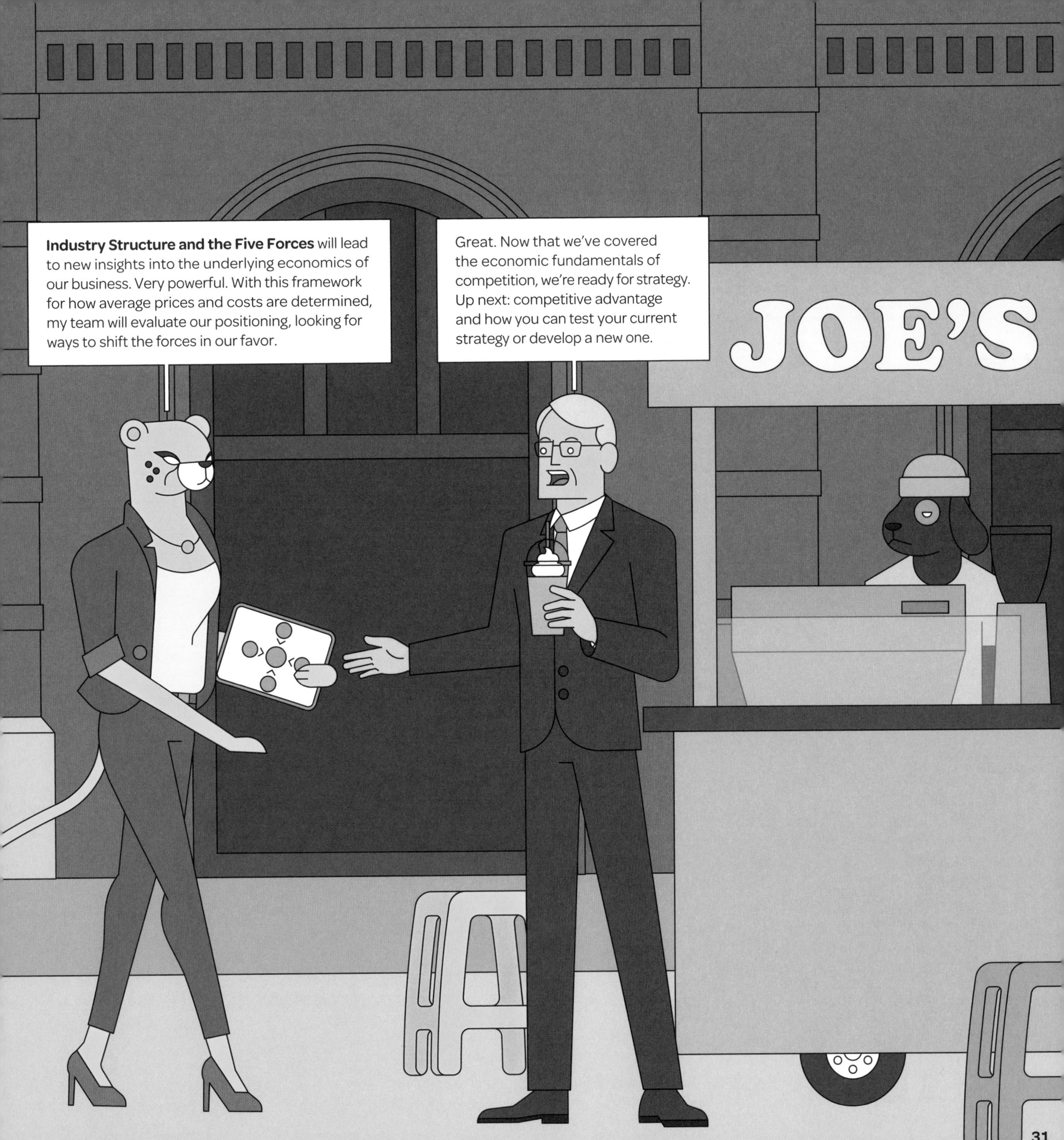
Industry Structure and the Five Forces will lead to new insights into the underlying economics of our business. Very powerful. With this framework for how average prices and costs are determined, my team will evaluate our positioning, looking for ways to shift the forces in our favor.
Great. Now that we've covered the economic fundamentals of competition, we're ready for strategy. Up next: competitive advantage and how you can test your current strategy or develop a new one.
JOE'S

SO, DOES ACORN HAVE A COMPETITIVE ADVANTAGE?

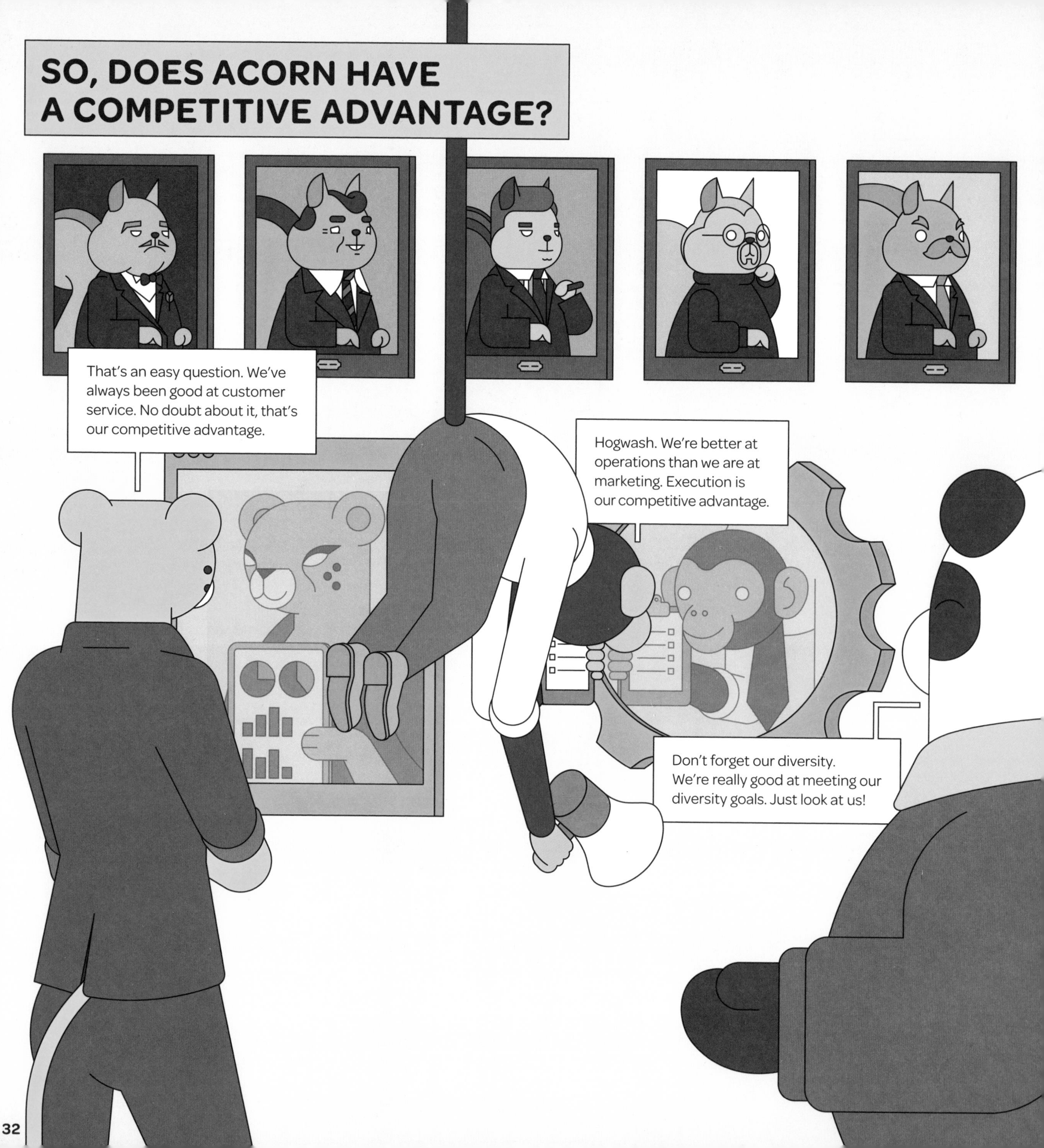
That's an easy question. We've always been good at customer service. No doubt about it, that's our competitive advantage.
Hogwash. We're better at operations than we are at marketing. Execution is our competitive advantage.
Don't forget our diversity. We're really good at meeting our diversity goals. Just look at us!

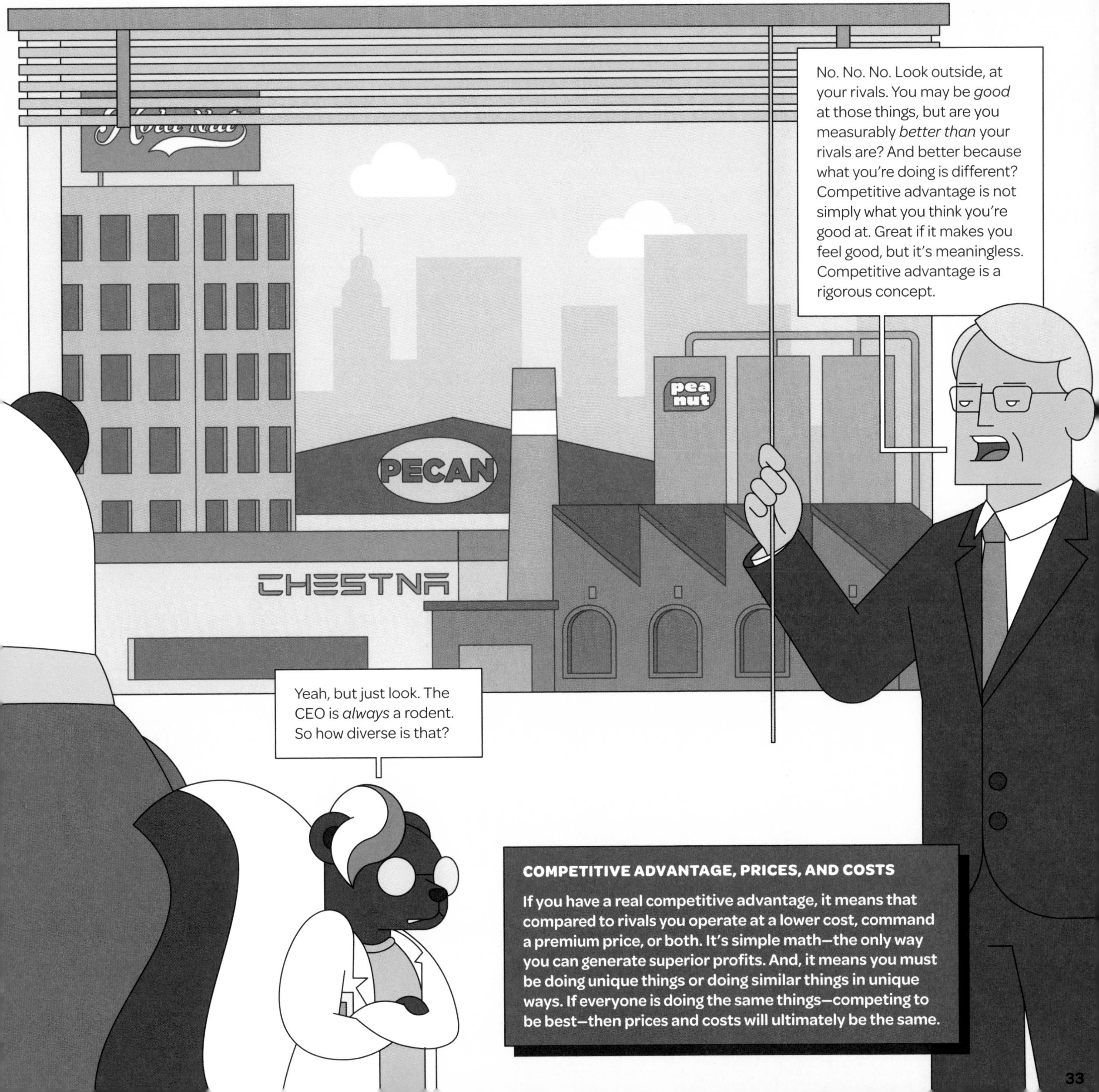
No. No. No. Look outside, at your rivals. You may be *good* at those things, but are you measurably *better than* your rivals are? And better because what you're doing is different? Competitive advantage is not simply what you think you're good at. Great if it makes you feel good, but it's meaningless. Competitive advantage is a rigorous concept.
Yeah, but just look. The CEO is *always* a rodent. So how diverse is that?
PECAN
pea nut
CHESTNA

COMPETITIVE ADVANTAGE, PRICES, AND COSTS

If you have a real competitive advantage, it means that compared to rivals you operate at a lower cost, command a premium price, or both. It's simple math—the only way you can generate superior profits. And, it means you must be doing unique things or doing similar things in unique ways. If everyone is doing the same things—competing to be best—then prices and costs will ultimately be the same.

COMPETITIVE ADVANTAGE AND THE VALUE CHAIN

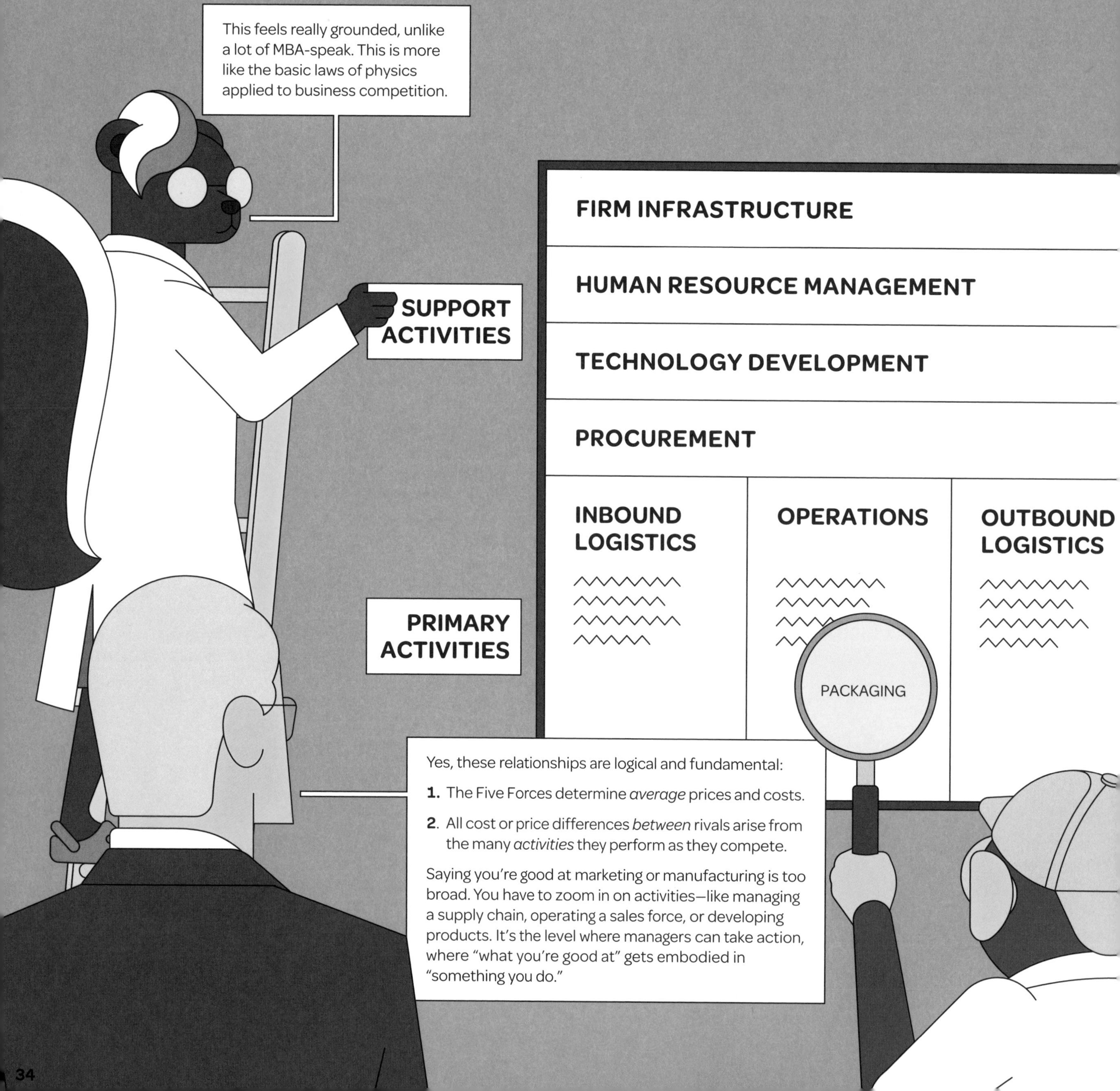
This feels really grounded, unlike a lot of MBA-speak. This is more like the basic laws of physics applied to business competition.
SUPPORT ACTIVITIES
PRIMARY ACTIVITIES
FIRM INFRASTRUCTURE
HUMAN RESOURCE MANAGEMENT
TECHNOLOGY DEVELOPMENT
PROCUREMENT
INBOUND LOGISTICS
OPERATIONS
OUTBOUND LOGISTICS
PACKAGING
Yes, these relationships are logical and fundamental:
1. The Five Forces determine *average* prices and costs.
2. All cost or price differences *between* rivals arise from the many *activities* they perform as they compete.
Saying you're good at marketing or manufacturing is too broad. You have to zoom in on activities—like managing a supply chain, operating a sales force, or developing products. It's the level where managers can take action, where "what you're good at" gets embodied in "something you do."

THE VALUE CHAIN

The *value chain* is a map of the operational activities a company performs to design, produce, sell, deliver, and support its products. It breaks down a company into its strategically relevant activities in order to focus on the sources of competitive advantage—the specific activities that result in premium prices or lower costs. A robust strategy will have distinctive approaches to primary functions (for example, product design or service delivery) and also to supporting activities (for example, talent development that focuses on the skills needed to deliver on the strategy). When you do this analysis, modify this generic configuration of the value chain to capture the relevant activities and the nature of competition in your industry.

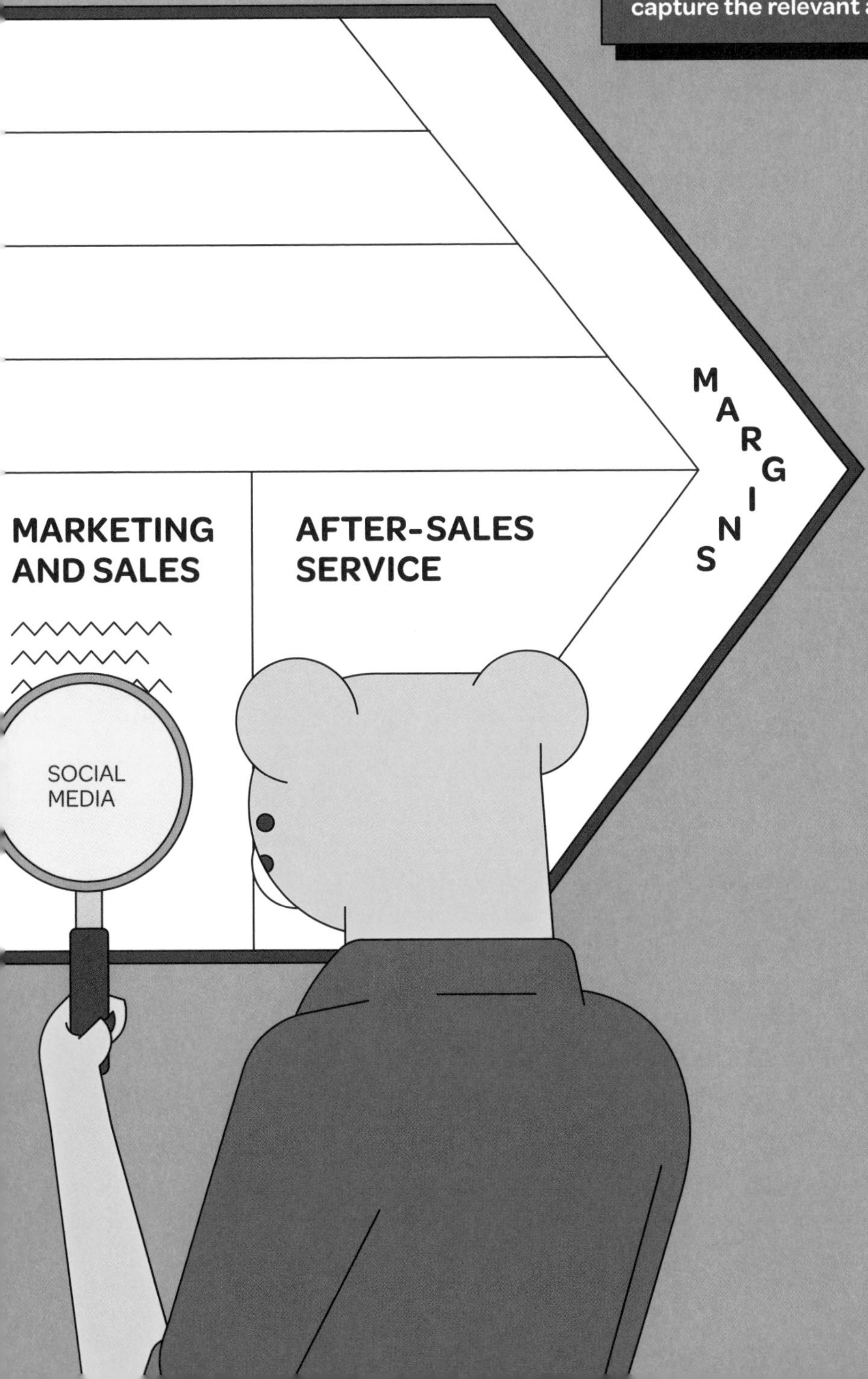

MARKETING AND SALES
AFTER-SALES SERVICE
SOCIAL MEDIA
MARGINS

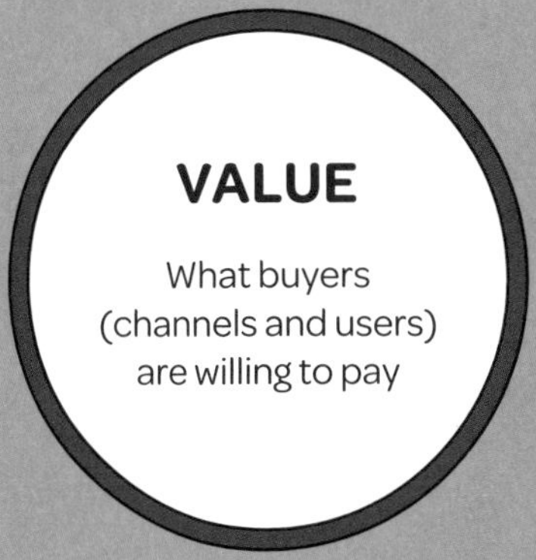

VALUE
What buyers (channels and users) are willing to pay

THE VALUE SYSTEM

Every value chain fits into a larger *value system*: all of the activities—regardless of who performs them—needed to create value for the end user. A company's value chain is typically just a part of a larger value system that includes the value chains of companies either upstream or downstream or both. It's important to see how your activities connect with those of your suppliers, channels, and customers.

VALUE CHAIN ANALYSIS: THE AUTO INDUSTRY

First, lay out the industry's major value-creating activities. Depending on the industry—and on each player's strategy—some activities will be more important to competitive advantage. Look for differences among rivals. Identify differentiators, activities that allow you to charge a higher price. Look for cost drivers, activities representing a large or growing percentage of costs where you can find new efficiencies. Your relative cost position (RCP) is built up from the cumulative cost of performing all the activities in the value chain.

DESIGN AND DEVELOPMENT

SOURCING

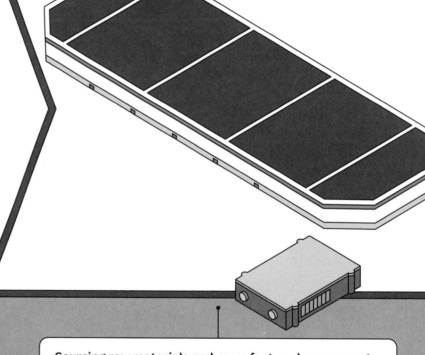

Design and development. How far upstream do the industry's activities extend? BMW's technological edge has been essential to its premium-brand pricing. Today the industry is facing enormous challenges in developing electric and self-driving vehicles.

Sourcing raw materials and manufactured components. The auto industry relies heavily on purchased inputs, making supply-chain management and some make-versus-buy decisions critical. Traditional car companies have outsourced batteries from third-party suppliers, but Tesla, seeking an early performance advantage in electric vehicles, joined with Panasonic to build the largest battery factory in the world.

Wow. This is a brilliant way to see how value is actually created. It forces you to think about how there are different ways of configuring the value chain in the same industry—and how those choices provide the tangible basis of competitive advantage. That's powerful.

PRODUCTION

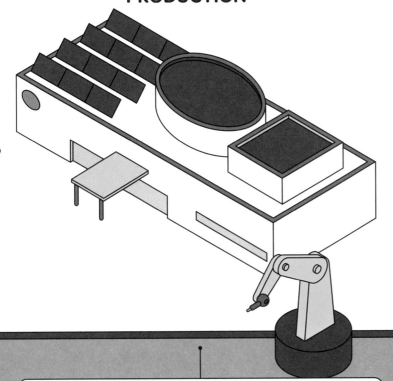

MARKETING, SALES, DISTRIBUTION

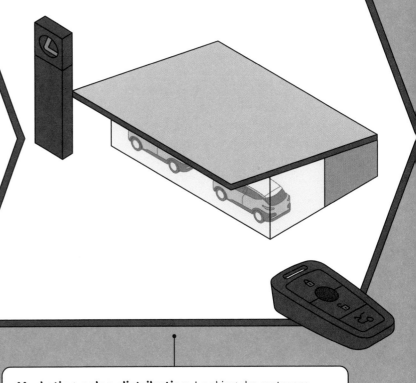

Product choices and production. What products and services are offered? And then, how are they made? Detroit once allowed customers to pick and choose from a long list of vehicle options, resulting in highly customized cars. That meant Detroit had to manufacture (and hold inventory for) literally hundreds of configurations of each model. Toyota's early innovations—dramatically limiting the complexity of its offerings coupled with its just-in-time production system—yielded cost and quality advantages, which lasted for many years as rivals struggled to copy these activities.

Marketing, sales, distribution. Looking downstream, how does the industry market, sell, distribute, deliver? Financing and after-sales service are part of the value the auto industry creates for customers. Unlike many rivals, Tesla is building its own dealer network to better support its Internet of Things (IoT) technology and its premium pricing, as Toyota did when it created its high-end Lexus brand.

ROBUST STRATEGIES: THE FIVE TESTS

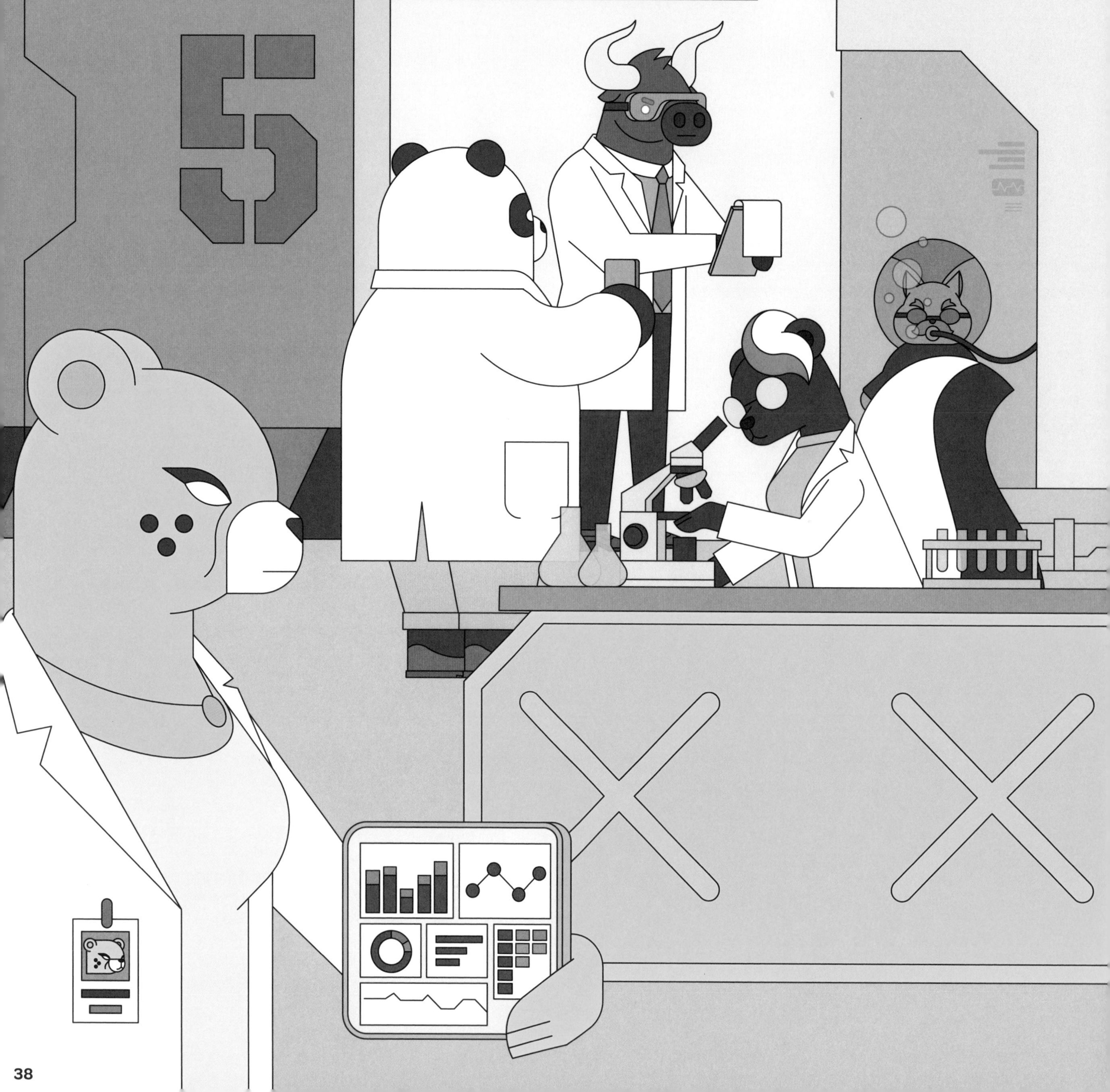
5

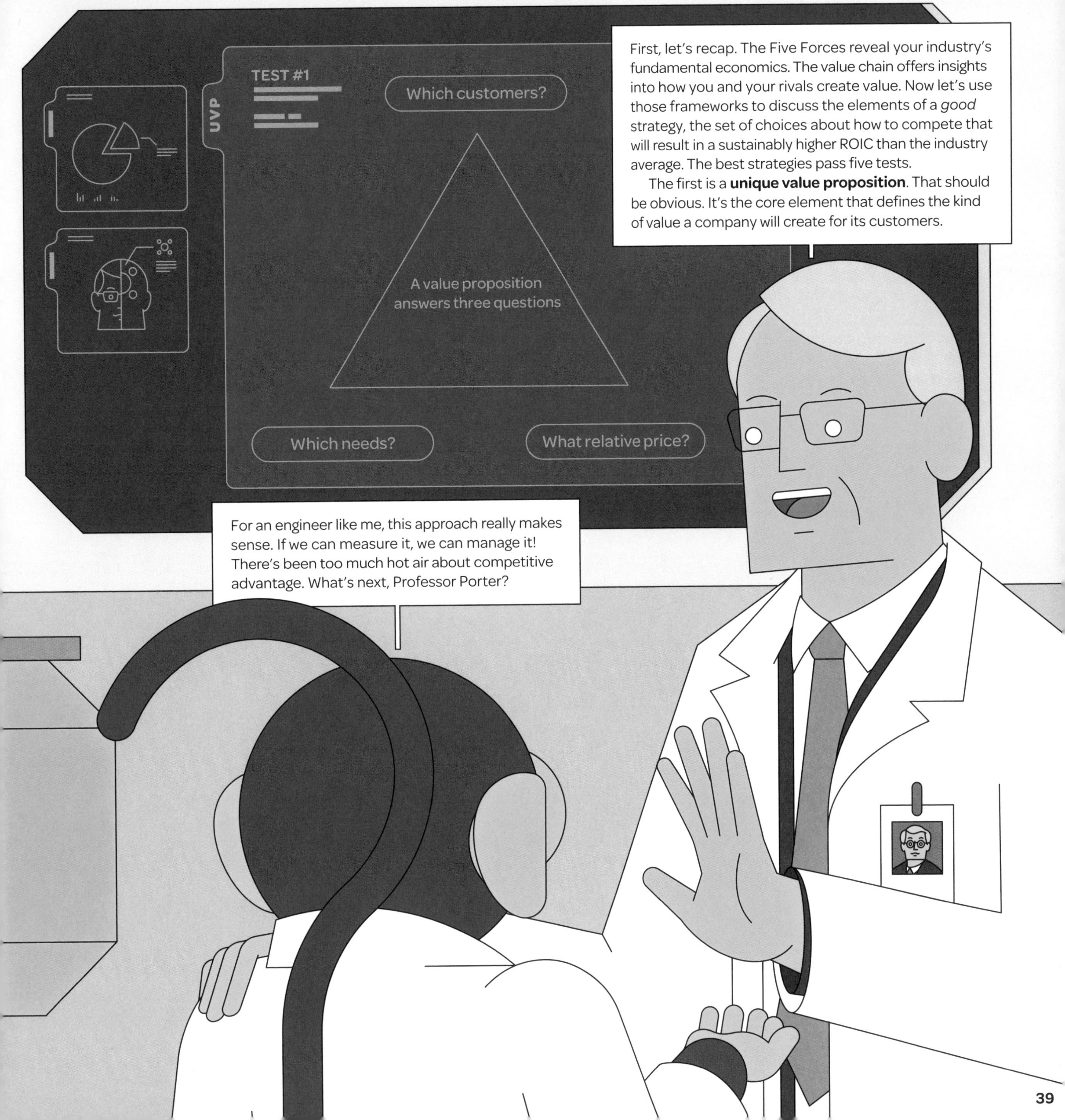
First, let's recap. The Five Forces reveal your industry's fundamental economics. The value chain offers insights into how you and your rivals create value. Now let's use those frameworks to discuss the elements of a *good* strategy, the set of choices about how to compete that will result in a sustainably higher ROIC than the industry average. The best strategies pass five tests.
The first is a **unique value proposition**. That should be obvious. It's the core element that defines the kind of value a company will create for its customers.
UVP
TEST #1
Which customers?
A value proposition answers three questions
Which needs?
What relative price?
For an engineer like me, this approach really makes sense. If we can measure it, we can manage it! There's been too much hot air about competitive advantage. What's next, Professor Porter?

TEST #1: WHICH CUSTOMERS?

A value proposition starts with the choice of which one or more distinct customer groups or segments to serve. Walmart's founder, Sam Walton, initially chose to serve customers in isolated rural towns—a geographic segmentation reflecting unmet needs in those areas. By avoiding direct rivalry with other discounters, Walmart gained time to hone its positioning as a retailer with everyday low prices able to serve a very broad customer base.

As we saw, PACCAR's target customer has been the individual owner-operator whose truck is his home away from home. In a price-competitive industry driven by large trucking companies, PACCAR has chosen small customers willing to pay a 10% price premium for a slew of custom product features—a luxurious sleeper cabin, for example—and services that make them more successful, like roadside assistance.

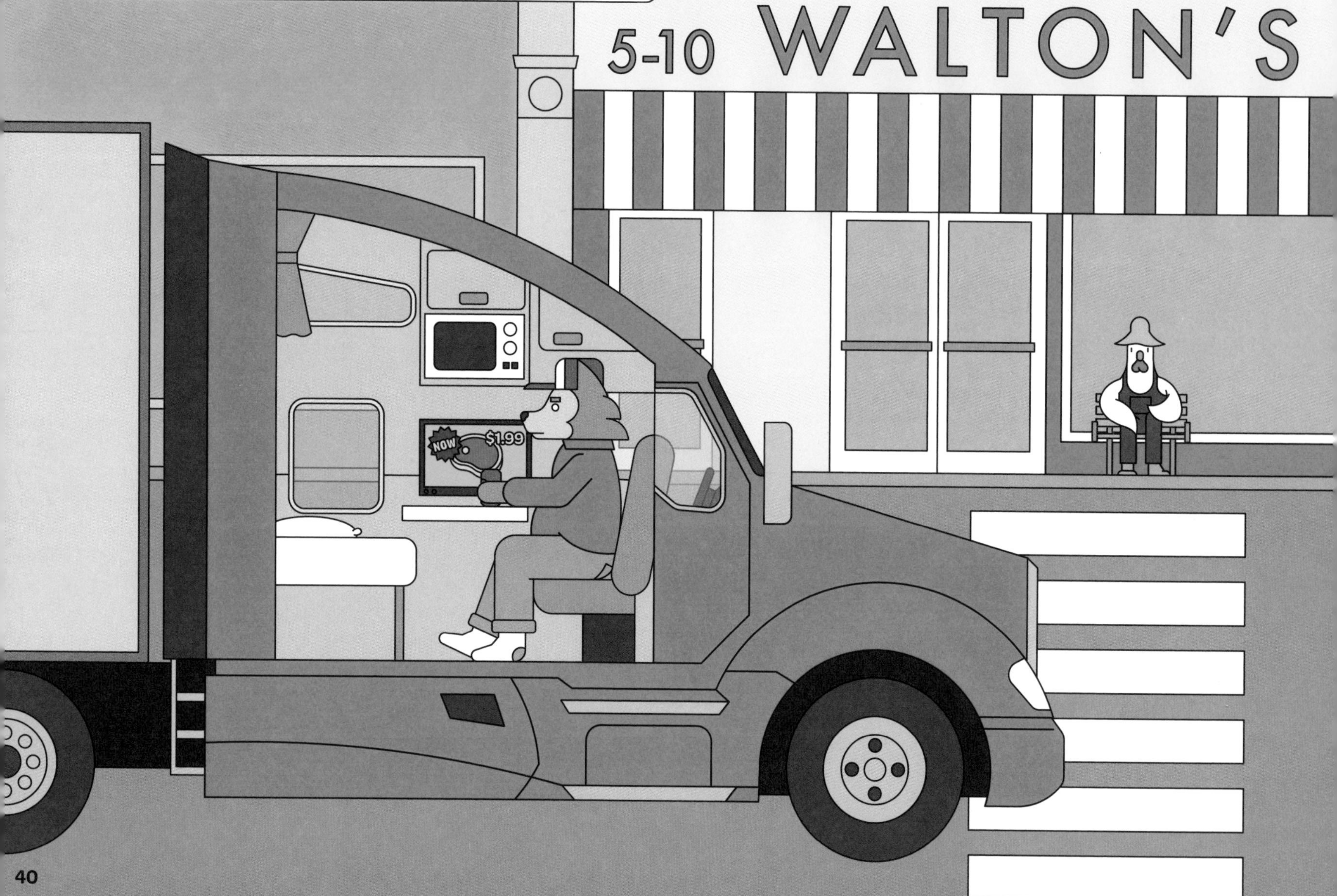
5-10 WALTON'S
NOW
$1.99

TEST #1: WHICH NEEDS?

Some value propositions are built around a unique ability to meet a particular need or a subset of needs. Customers who share the same needs don't necessarily belong to the same demographic category.

When Southwest Airlines first appeared on the scene, it successfully served two seemingly incompatible customer groups. Its short-haul, point-to-point routes appealed to businesspeople seeking the convenience of frequent flights as well as to budget travelers who now could afford to fly instead of taking the bus or driving.

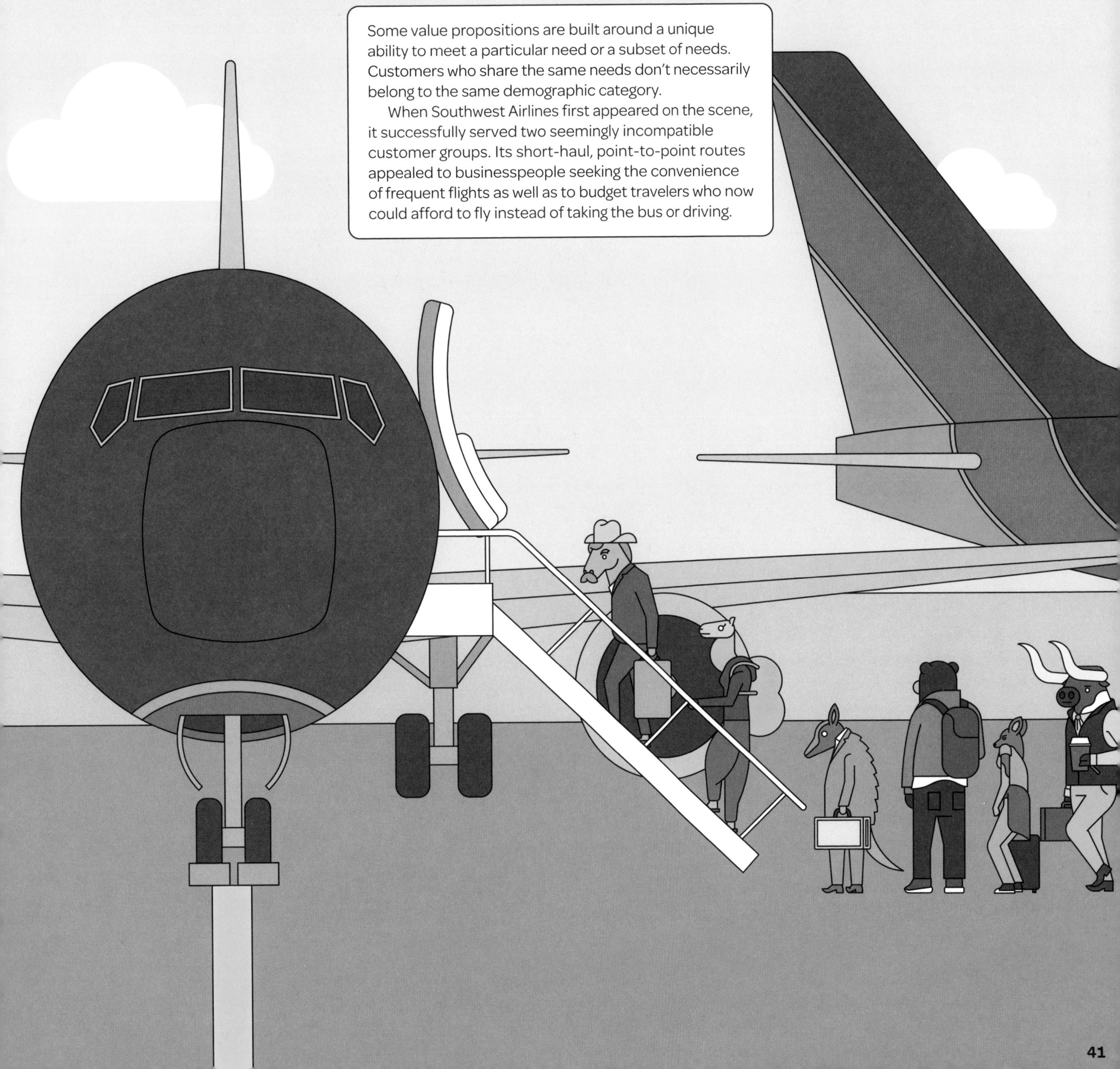

TEST #1: WHAT RELATIVE PRICE?

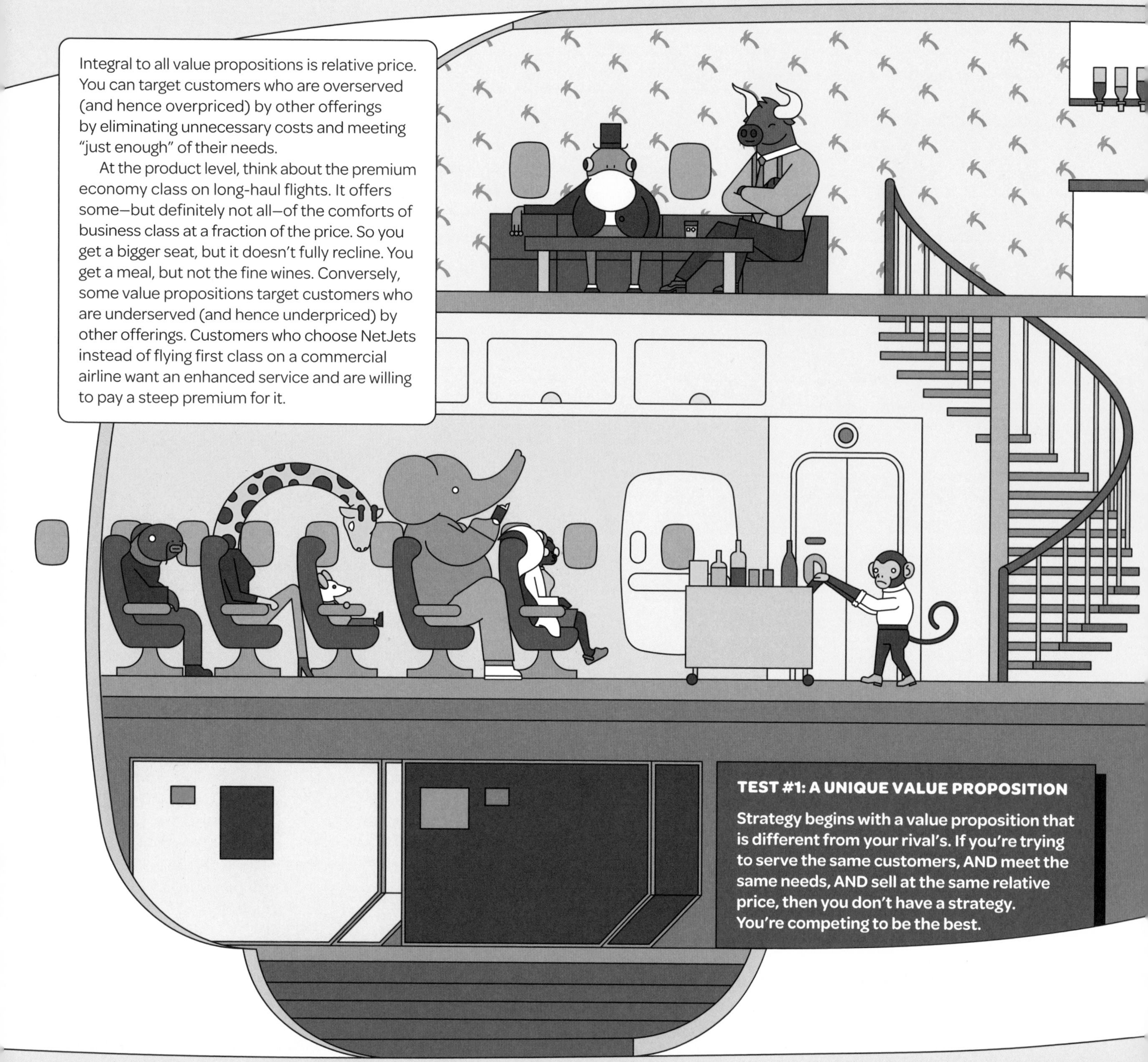

Integral to all value propositions is relative price. You can target customers who are overserved (and hence overpriced) by other offerings by eliminating unnecessary costs and meeting "just enough" of their needs.

At the product level, think about the premium economy class on long-haul flights. It offers some—but definitely not all—of the comforts of business class at a fraction of the price. So you get a bigger seat, but it doesn't fully recline. You get a meal, but not the fine wines. Conversely, some value propositions target customers who are underserved (and hence underpriced) by other offerings. Customers who choose NetJets instead of flying first class on a commercial airline want an enhanced service and are willing to pay a steep premium for it.

TEST #1: A UNIQUE VALUE PROPOSITION

Strategy begins with a value proposition that is different from your rival's. If you're trying to serve the same customers, AND meet the same needs, AND sell at the same relative price, then you don't have a strategy. You're competing to be the best.

TEST #2: A TAILORED VALUE CHAIN

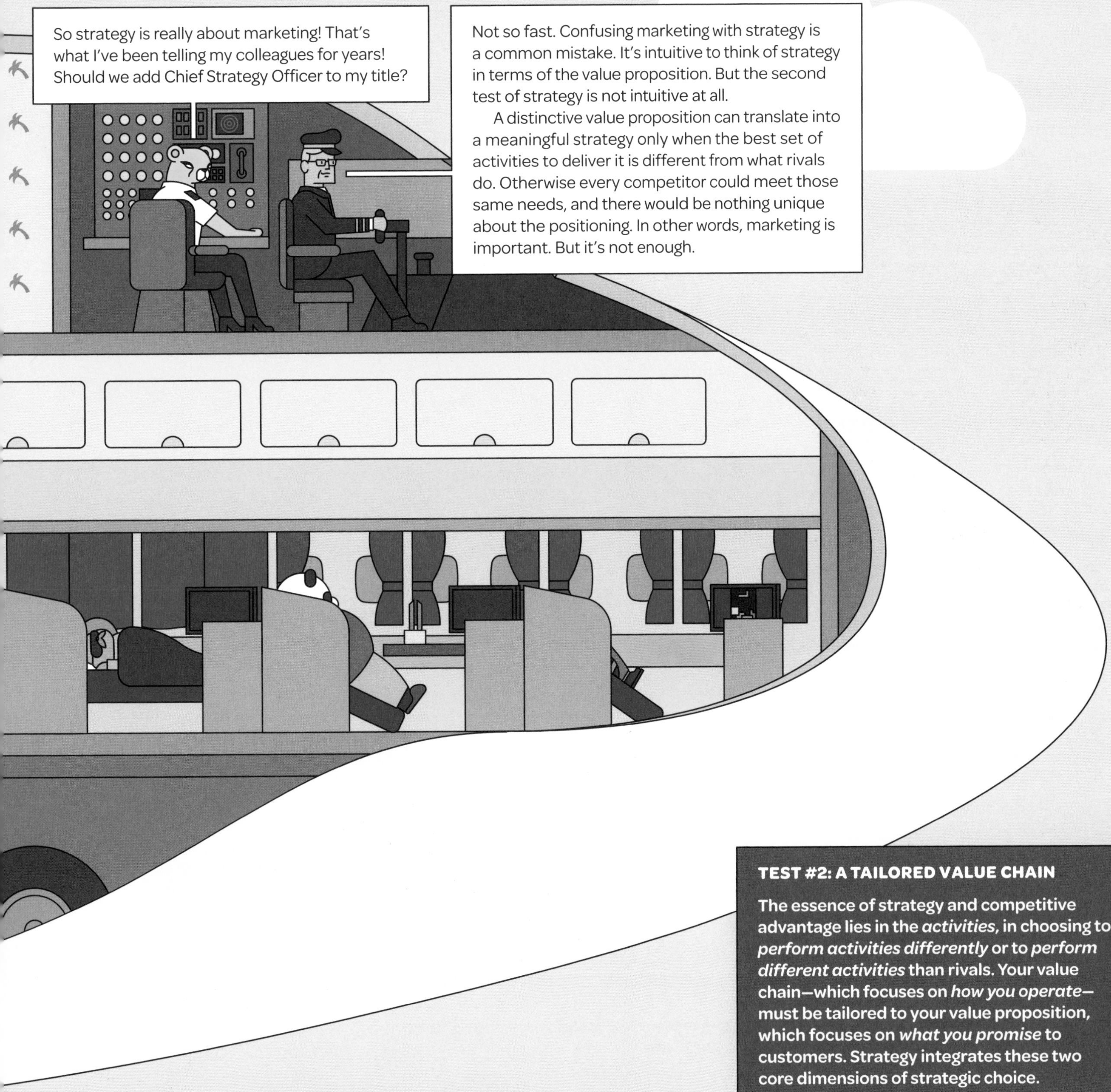
So strategy is really about marketing! That's what I've been telling my colleagues for years! Should we add Chief Strategy Officer to my title?
Not so fast. Confusing marketing with strategy is a common mistake. It's intuitive to think of strategy in terms of the value proposition. But the second test of strategy is not intuitive at all.
A distinctive value proposition can translate into a meaningful strategy only when the best set of activities to deliver it is different from what rivals do. Otherwise every competitor could meet those same needs, and there would be nothing unique about the positioning. In other words, marketing is important. But it's not enough.

TEST #2: A TAILORED VALUE CHAIN

The essence of strategy and competitive advantage lies in the *activities*, in choosing to *perform activities differently* or to *perform different activities* than rivals. Your value chain—which focuses on *how you operate*—must be tailored to your value proposition, which focuses on *what you promise* to customers. Strategy integrates these two core dimensions of strategic choice.

IKEA'S TAILORED VALUE CHAIN

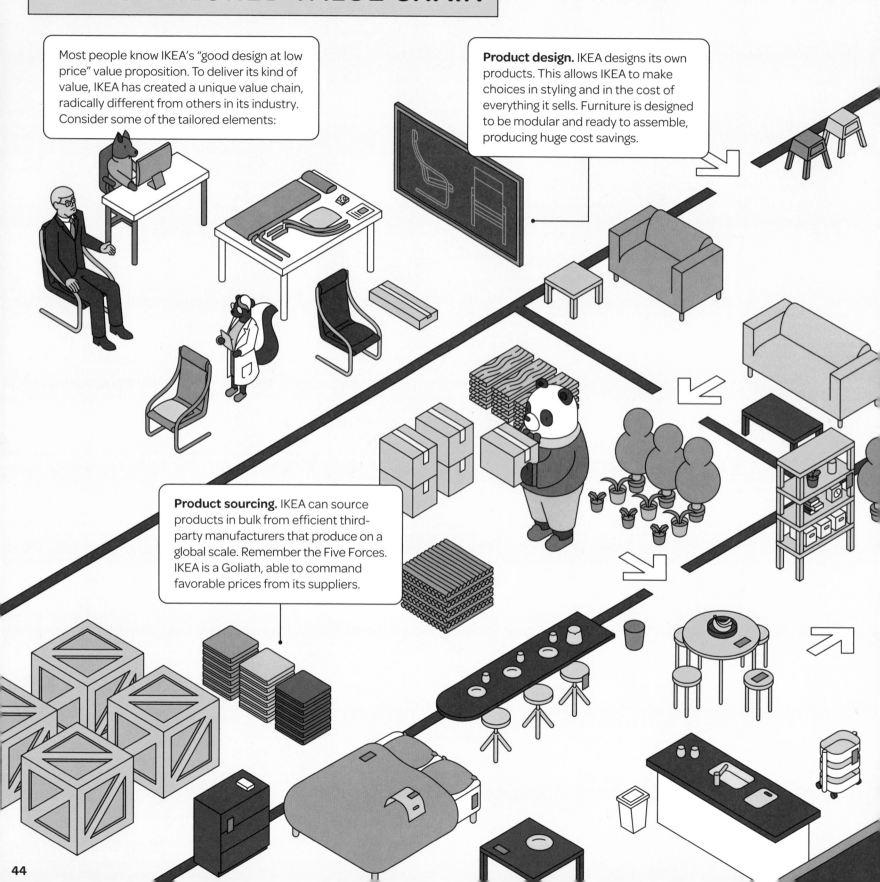

Most people know IKEA's "good design at low price" value proposition. To deliver its kind of value, IKEA has created a unique value chain, radically different from others in its industry. Consider some of the tailored elements:

Product design. IKEA designs its own products. This allows IKEA to make choices in styling and in the cost of everything it sells. Furniture is designed to be modular and ready to assemble, producing huge cost savings.

Product sourcing. IKEA can source products in bulk from efficient third-party manufacturers that produce on a global scale. Remember the Five Forces. IKEA is a Goliath, able to command favorable prices from its suppliers.

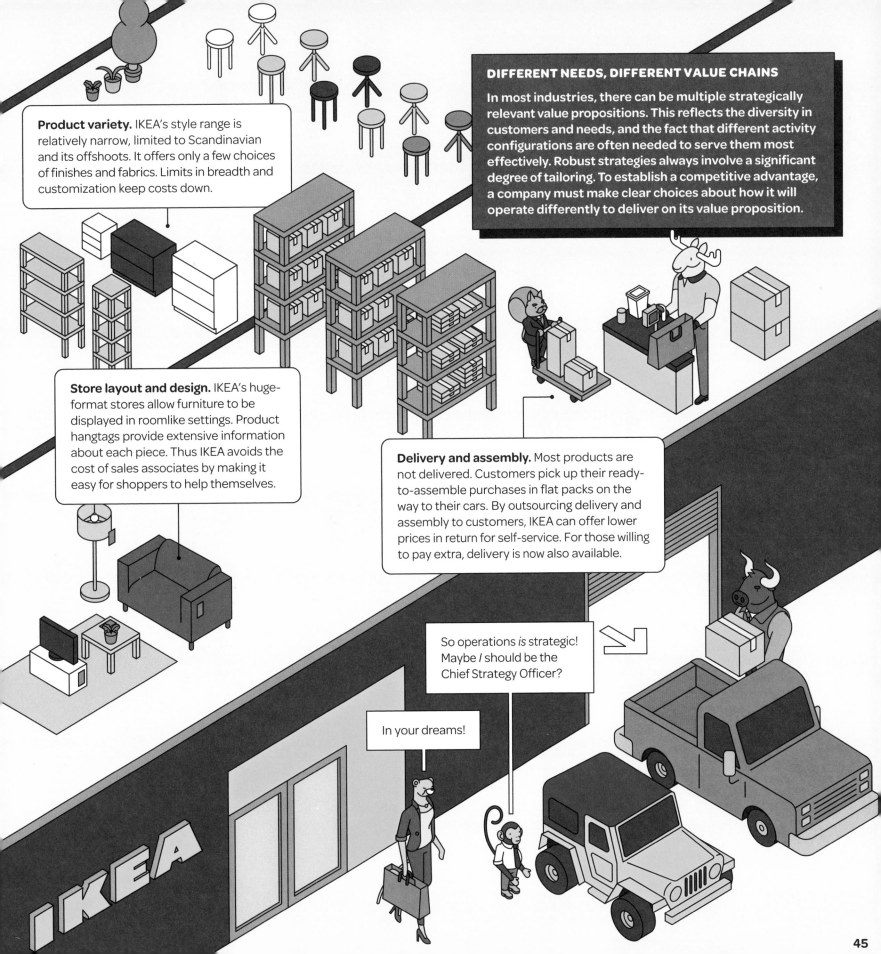

Product variety. IKEA's style range is relatively narrow, limited to Scandinavian and its offshoots. It offers only a few choices of finishes and fabrics. Limits in breadth and customization keep costs down.

DIFFERENT NEEDS, DIFFERENT VALUE CHAINS

In most industries, there can be multiple strategically relevant value propositions. This reflects the diversity in customers and needs, and the fact that different activity configurations are often needed to serve them most effectively. Robust strategies always involve a significant degree of tailoring. To establish a competitive advantage, a company must make clear choices about how it will operate differently to deliver on its value proposition.

Store layout and design. IKEA's huge-format stores allow furniture to be displayed in roomlike settings. Product hangtags provide extensive information about each piece. Thus IKEA avoids the cost of sales associates by making it easy for shoppers to help themselves.

Delivery and assembly. Most products are not delivered. Customers pick up their ready-to-assemble purchases in flat packs on the way to their cars. By outsourcing delivery and assembly to customers, IKEA can offer lower prices in return for self-service. For those willing to pay extra, delivery is now also available.

So operations *is* strategic! Maybe *I* should be the Chief Strategy Officer?

In your dreams!

IKEA

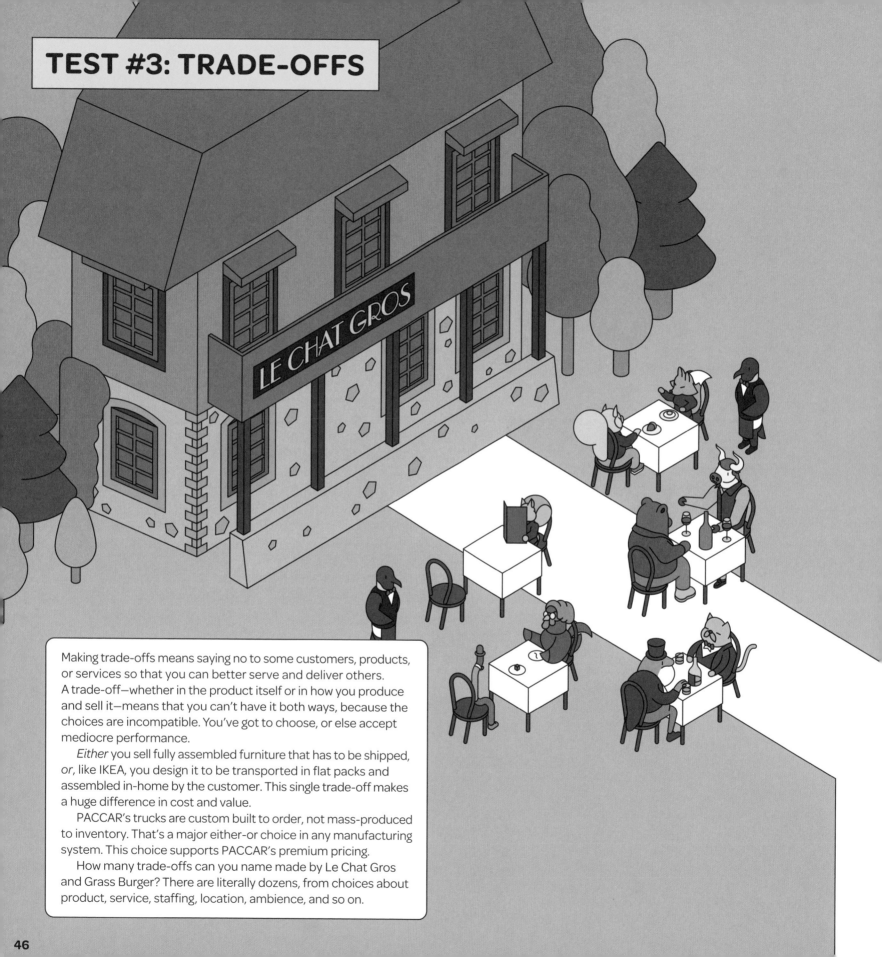

TEST #3: TRADE-OFFS

Making trade-offs means saying no to some customers, products, or services so that you can better serve and deliver others. A trade-off—whether in the product itself or in how you produce and sell it—means that you can't have it both ways, because the choices are incompatible. You've got to choose, or else accept mediocre performance.

Either you sell fully assembled furniture that has to be shipped, *or*, like IKEA, you design it to be transported in flat packs and assembled in-home by the customer. This single trade-off makes a huge difference in cost and value.

PACCAR's trucks are custom built to order, not mass-produced to inventory. That's a major either-or choice in any manufacturing system. This choice supports PACCAR's premium pricing.

How many trade-offs can you name made by Le Chat Gros and Grass Burger? There are literally dozens, from choices about product, service, staffing, location, ambience, and so on.

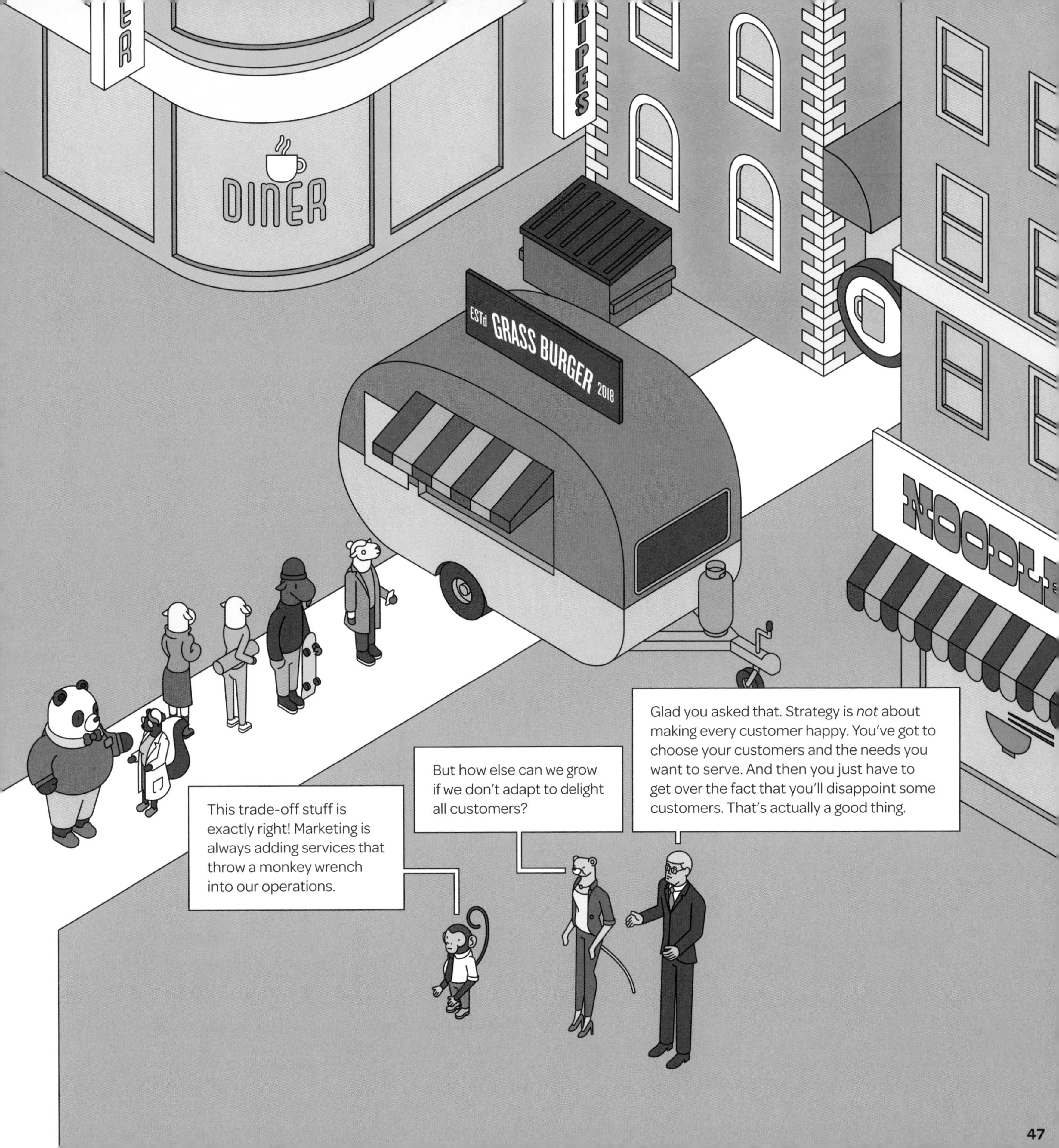
DINER
ESTd GRASS BURGER 2018
NOODLE
This trade-off stuff is exactly right! Marketing is always adding services that throw a monkey wrench into our operations.
But how else can we grow if we don't adapt to delight all customers?
Glad you asked that. Strategy is *not* about making every customer happy. You've got to choose your customers and the needs you want to serve. And then you just have to get over the fact that you'll disappoint some customers. That's actually a good thing.

TEST #3: TRADE-OFFS—WHEN TO SAY NO

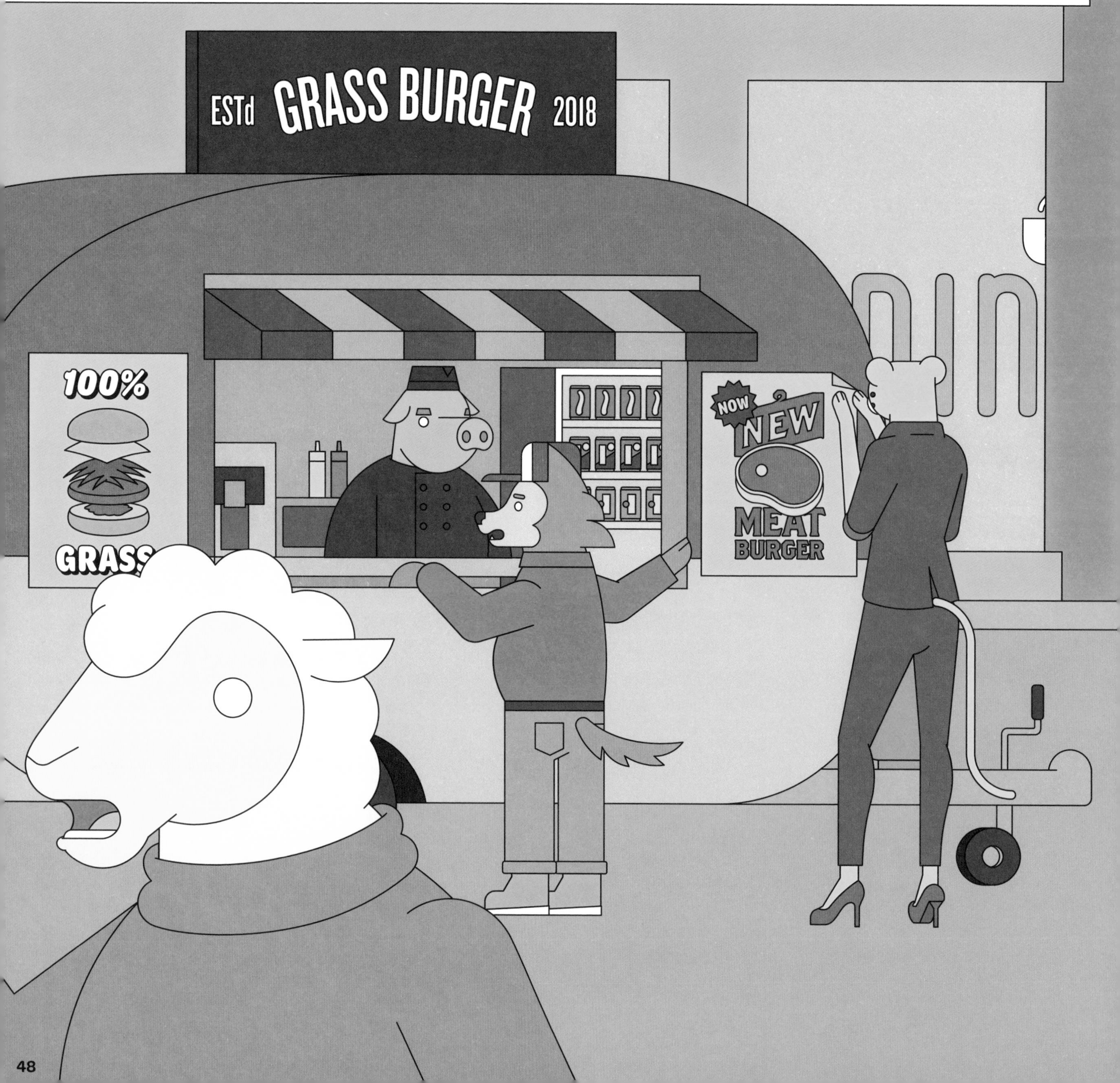

ESTd GRASS BURGER 2018
100%
GRASS
NOW
NEW
MEAT
BURGER

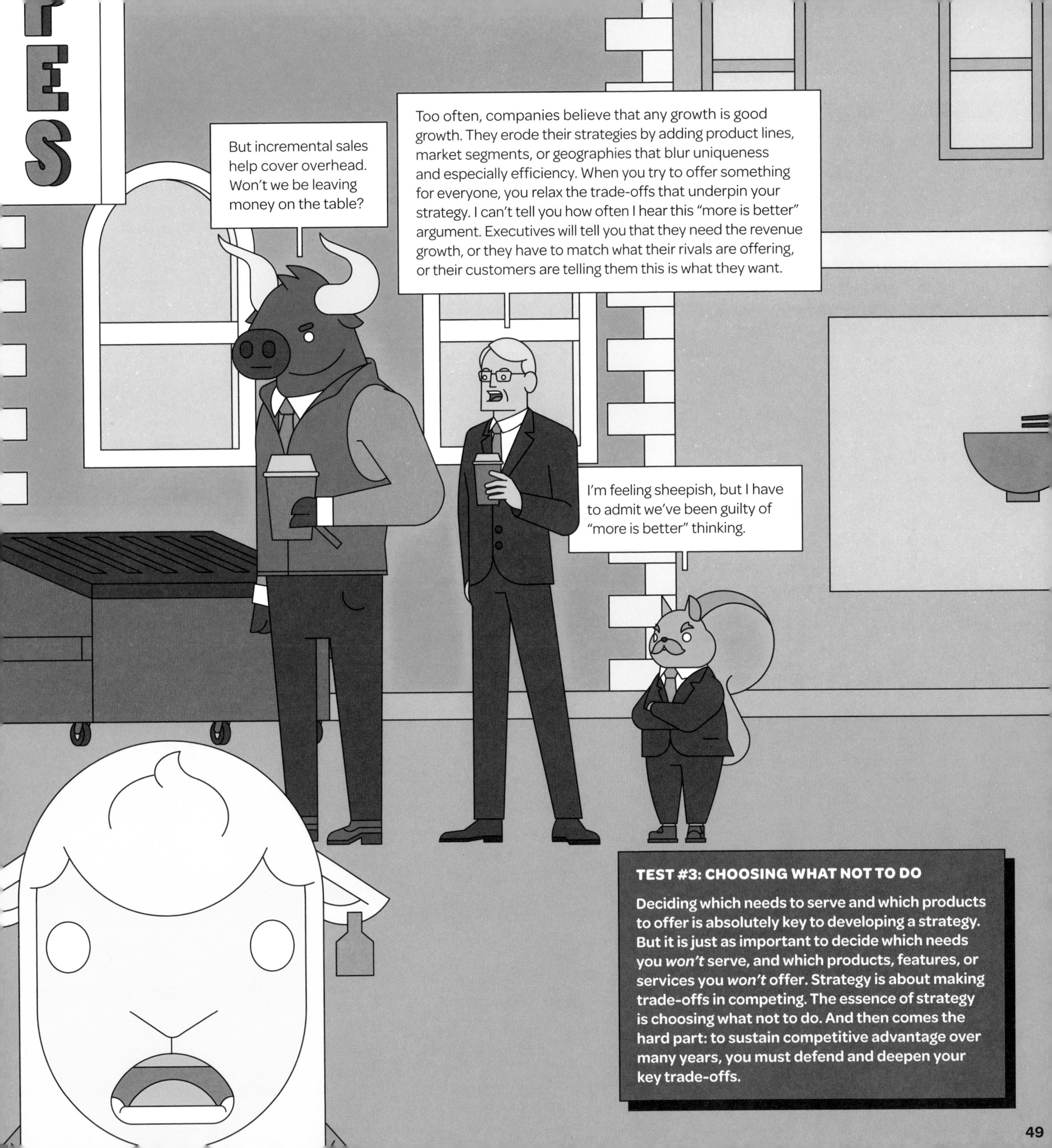
But incremental sales help cover overhead. Won't we be leaving money on the table?
Too often, companies believe that any growth is good growth. They erode their strategies by adding product lines, market segments, or geographies that blur uniqueness and especially efficiency. When you try to offer something for everyone, you relax the trade-offs that underpin your strategy. I can't tell you how often I hear this "more is better" argument. Executives will tell you that they need the revenue growth, or they have to match what their rivals are offering, or their customers are telling them this is what they want.
I'm feeling sheepish, but I have to admit we've been guilty of "more is better" thinking.

TEST #3: CHOOSING WHAT NOT TO DO

Deciding which needs to serve and which products to offer is absolutely key to developing a strategy. But it is just as important to decide which needs you *won't* serve, and which products, features, or services you *won't* offer. Strategy is about making trade-offs in competing. The essence of strategy is choosing what not to do. And then comes the hard part: to sustain competitive advantage over many years, you must defend and deepen your key trade-offs.

TEST #4: FIT

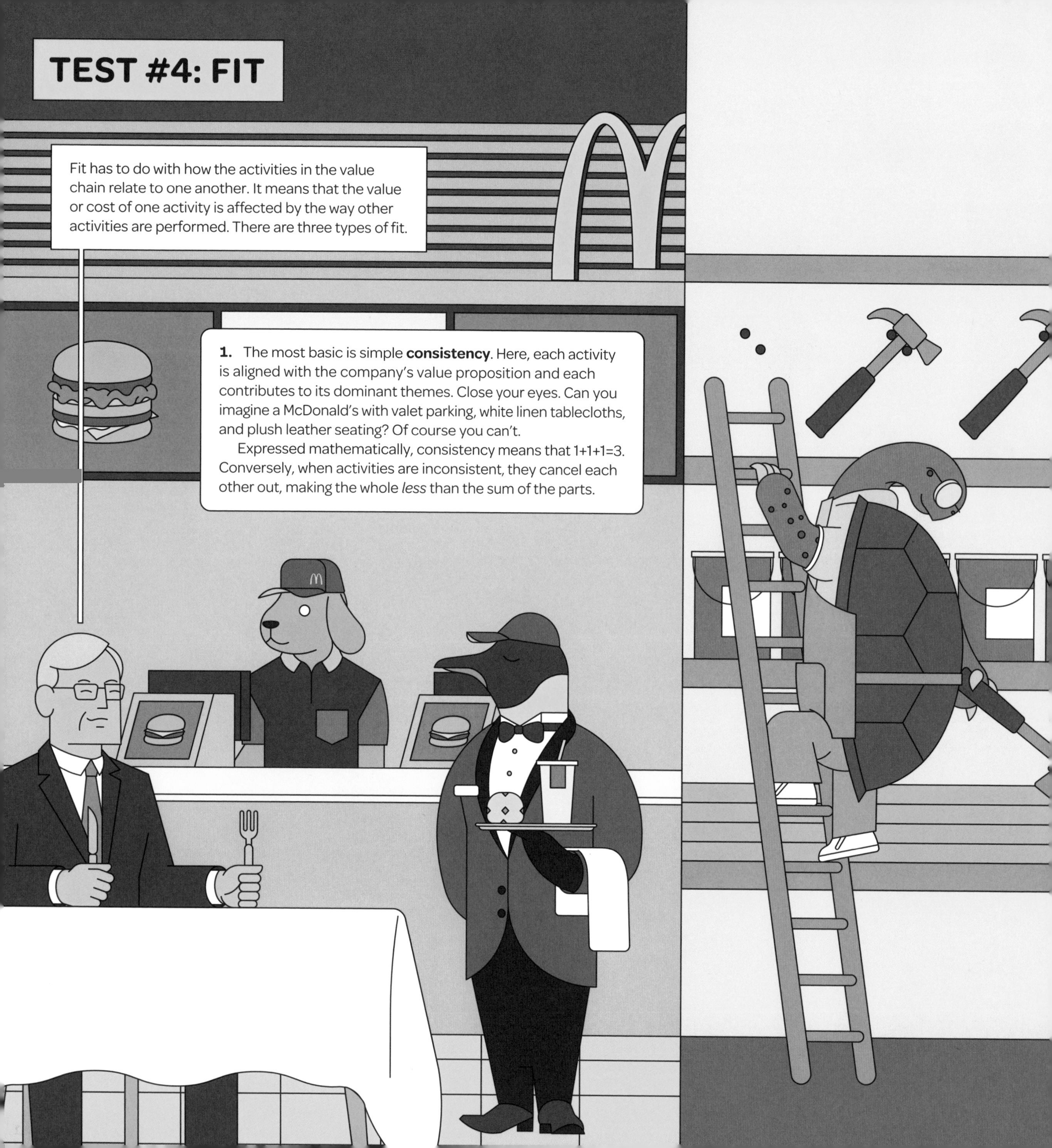

Fit has to do with how the activities in the value chain relate to one another. It means that the value or cost of one activity is affected by the way other activities are performed. There are three types of fit.

1. The most basic is simple **consistency**. Here, each activity is aligned with the company's value proposition and each contributes to its dominant themes. Close your eyes. Can you imagine a McDonald's with valet parking, white linen tablecloths, and plush leather seating? Of course you can't.

Expressed mathematically, consistency means that 1+1+1=3. Conversely, when activities are inconsistent, they cancel each other out, making the whole *less* than the sum of the parts.

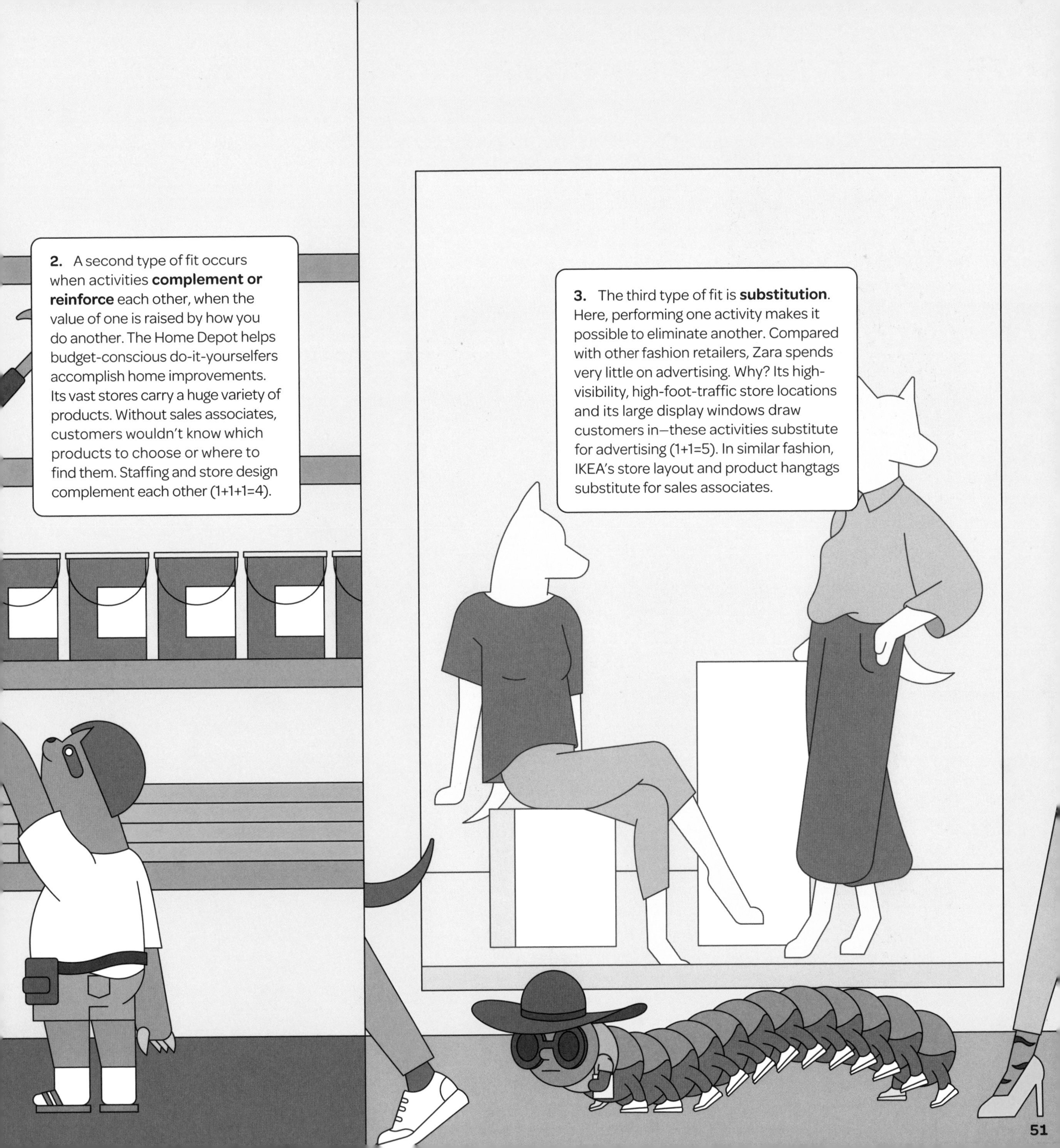

2. A second type of fit occurs when activities **complement or reinforce** each other, when the value of one is raised by how you do another. The Home Depot helps budget-conscious do-it-yourselfers accomplish home improvements. Its vast stores carry a huge variety of products. Without sales associates, customers wouldn't know which products to choose or where to find them. Staffing and store design complement each other (1+1+1=4).

3. The third type of fit is **substitution**. Here, performing one activity makes it possible to eliminate another. Compared with other fashion retailers, Zara spends very little on advertising. Why? Its high-visibility, high-foot-traffic store locations and its large display windows draw customers in—these activities substitute for advertising (1+1=5). In similar fashion, IKEA's store layout and product hangtags substitute for sales associates.

TEST #4: FIT AMPLIFIES COMPETITIVE ADVANTAGE

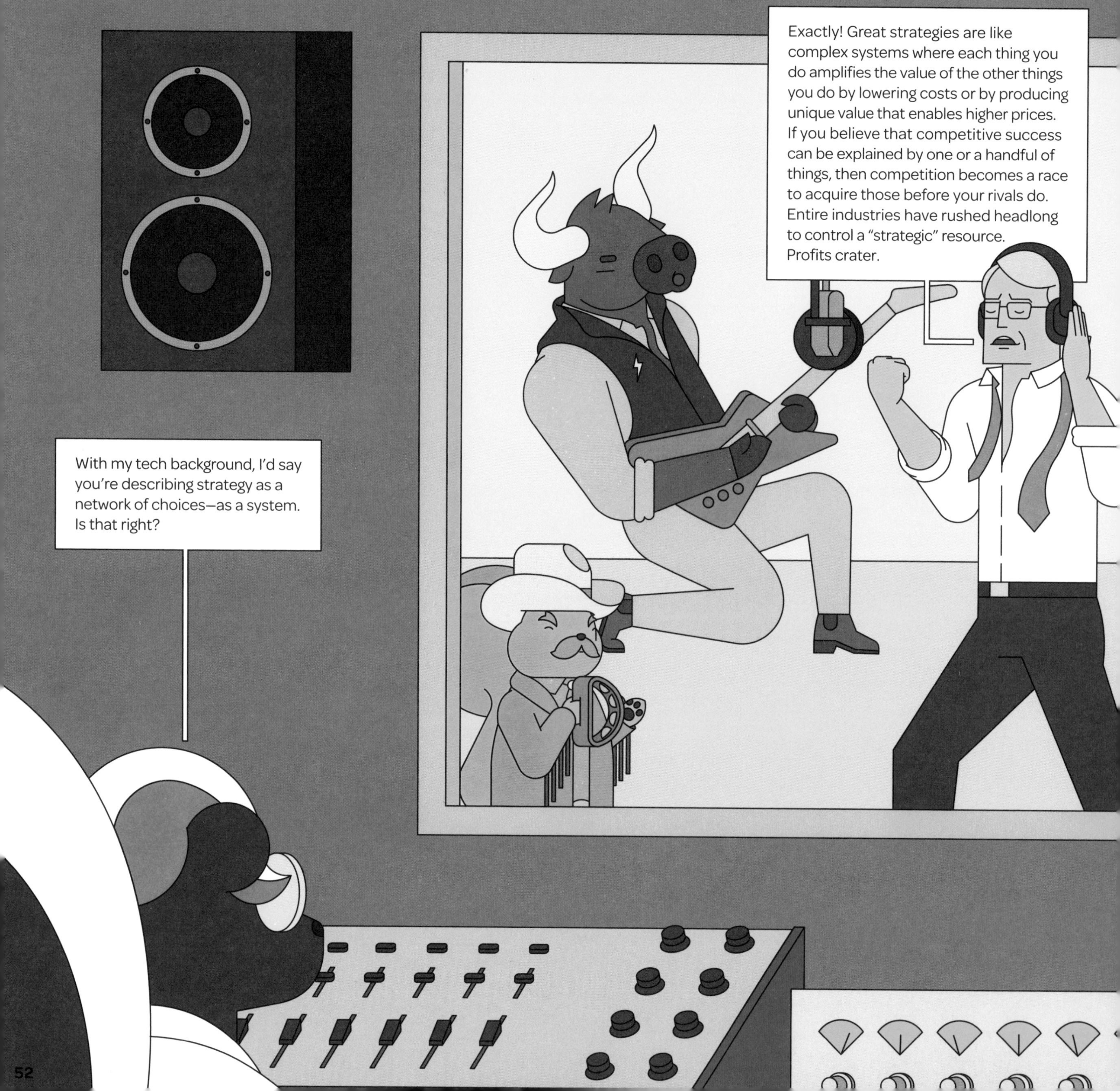

With my tech background, I'd say you're describing strategy as a network of choices—as a system. Is that right?
Exactly! Great strategies are like complex systems where each thing you do amplifies the value of the other things you do by lowering costs or by producing unique value that enables higher prices. If you believe that competitive success can be explained by one or a handful of things, then competition becomes a race to acquire those before your rivals do. Entire industries have rushed headlong to control a "strategic" resource. Profits crater.

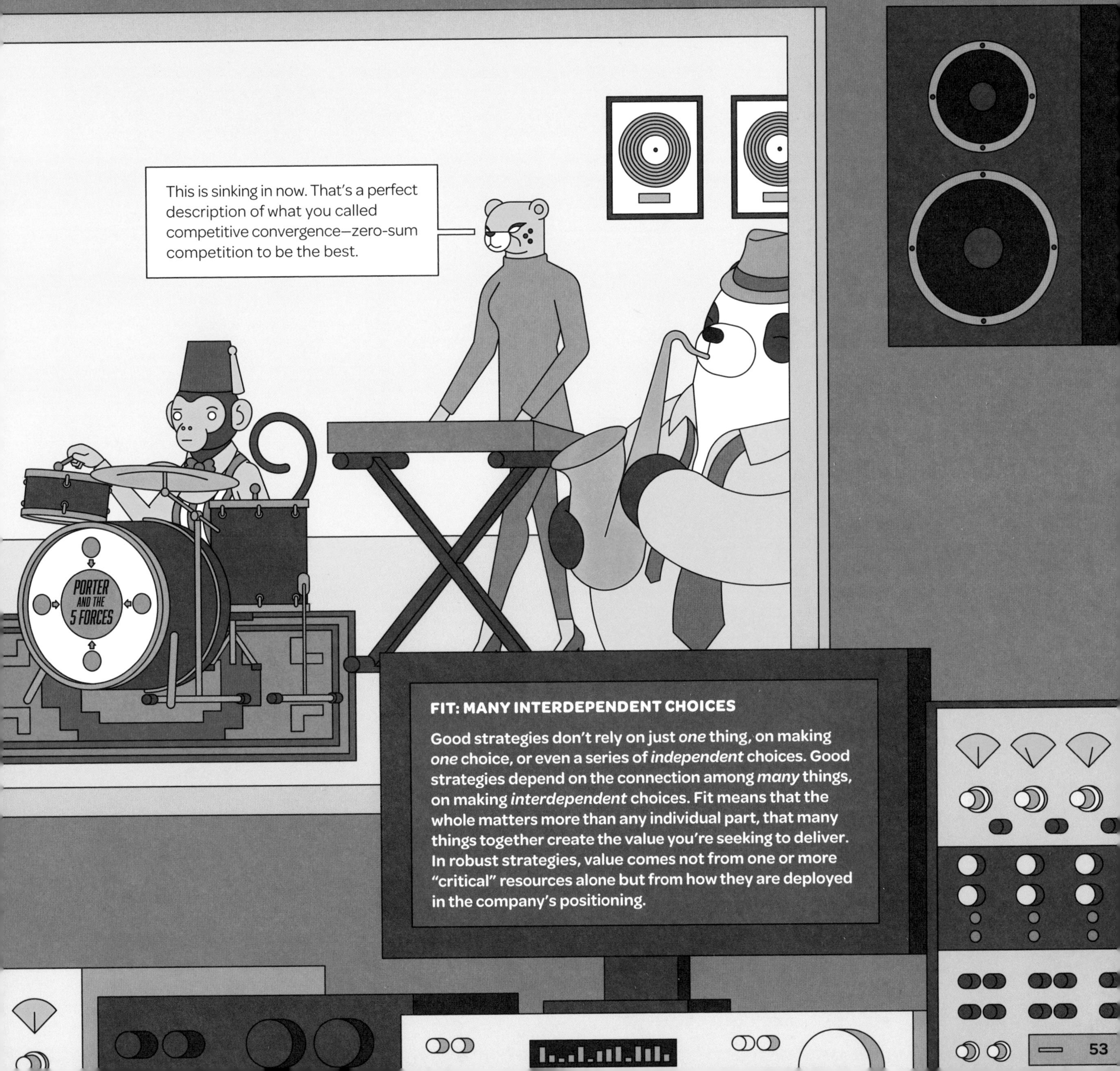
This is sinking in now. That's a perfect description of what you called competitive convergence—zero-sum competition to be the best.
PORTER AND THE 5 FORCES

FIT: MANY INTERDEPENDENT CHOICES

Good strategies don't rely on just *one* thing, on making *one* choice, or even a series of *independent* choices. Good strategies depend on the connection among *many* things, on making *interdependent* choices. Fit means that the whole matters more than any individual part, that many things together create the value you're seeking to deliver. In robust strategies, value comes not from one or more "critical" resources alone but from how they are deployed in the company's positioning.

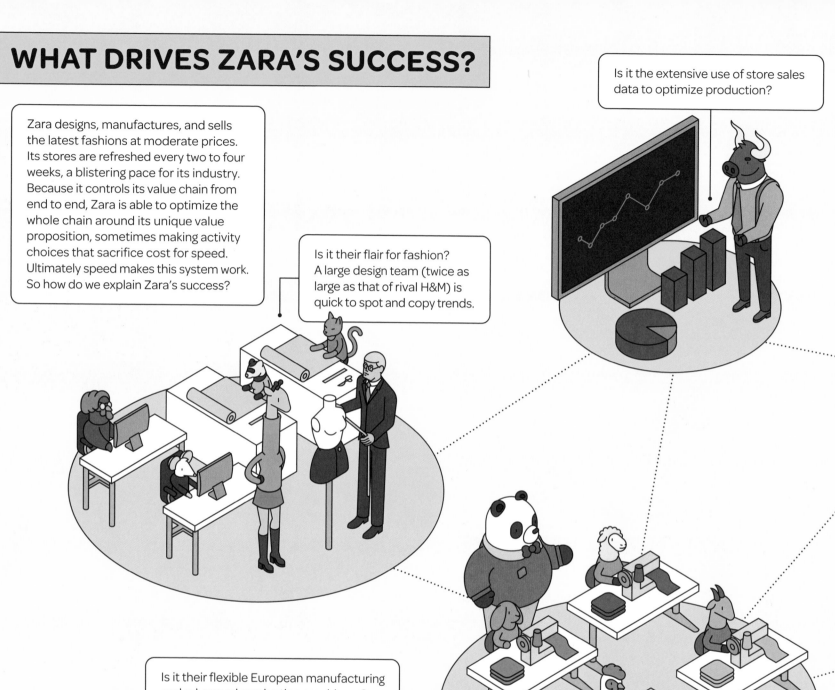

WHAT DRIVES ZARA'S SUCCESS?

Zara designs, manufactures, and sells the latest fashions at moderate prices. Its stores are refreshed every two to four weeks, a blistering pace for its industry. Because it controls its value chain from end to end, Zara is able to optimize the whole chain around its unique value proposition, sometimes making activity choices that sacrifice cost for speed. Ultimately speed makes this system work. So how do we explain Zara's success?

Is it their flair for fashion? A large design team (twice as large as that of rival H&M) is quick to spot and copy trends.

Is it the extensive use of store sales data to optimize production?

Is it their flexible European manufacturing and advanced production machinery? Its rivals have long lead times from outsourced, lower-cost Asian production.

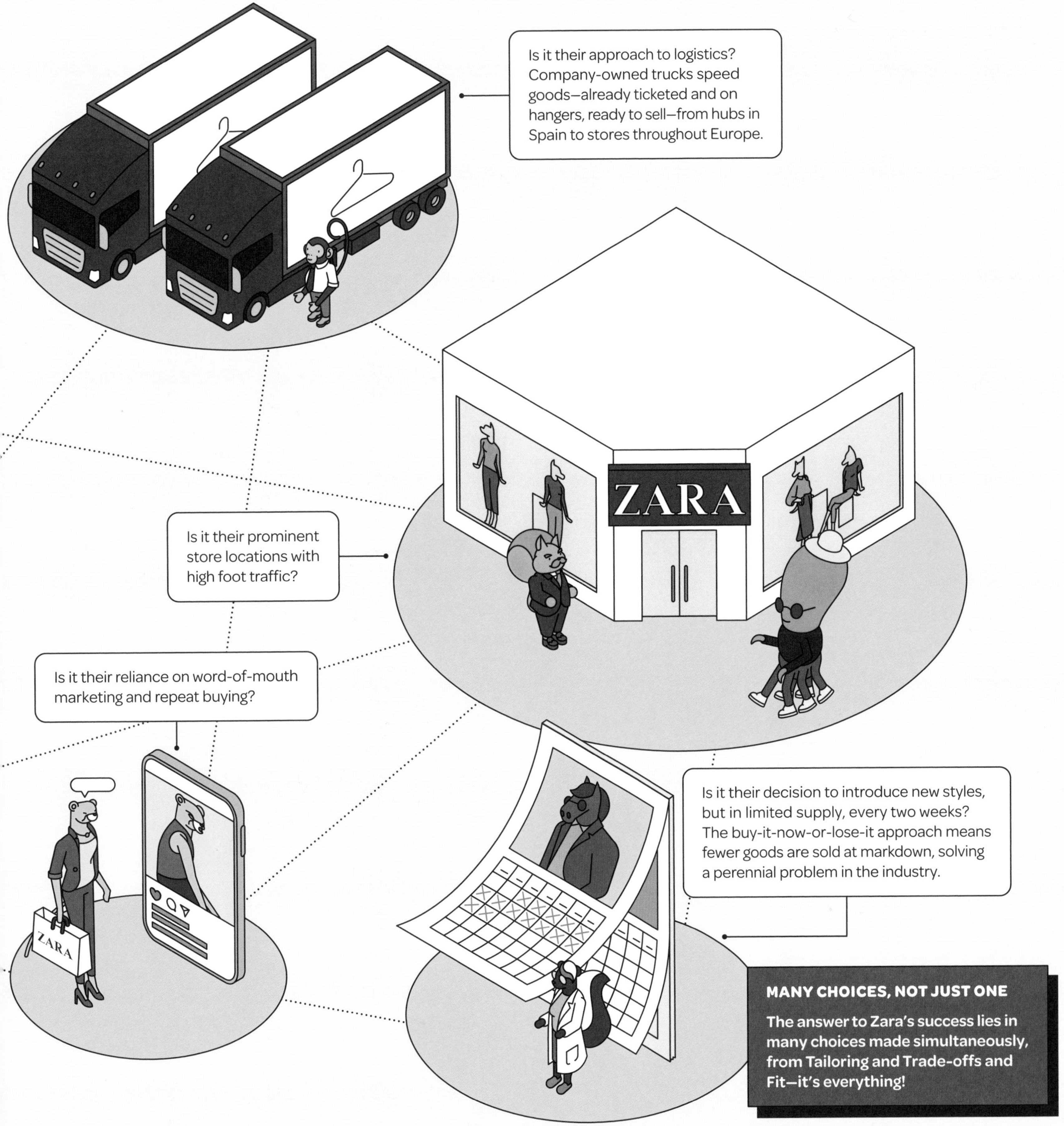
Is it their approach to logistics? Company-owned trucks speed goods—already ticketed and on hangers, ready to sell—from hubs in Spain to stores throughout Europe.
ZARA
Is it their prominent store locations with high foot traffic?
Is it their reliance on word-of-mouth marketing and repeat buying?
ZARA
Is it their decision to introduce new styles, but in limited supply, every two weeks? The buy-it-now-or-lose-it approach means fewer goods are sold at markdown, solving a perennial problem in the industry.

MANY CHOICES, NOT JUST ONE

The answer to Zara's success lies in many choices made simultaneously, from Tailoring and Trade-offs and Fit—it's everything!

TEST #5: CONTINUITY

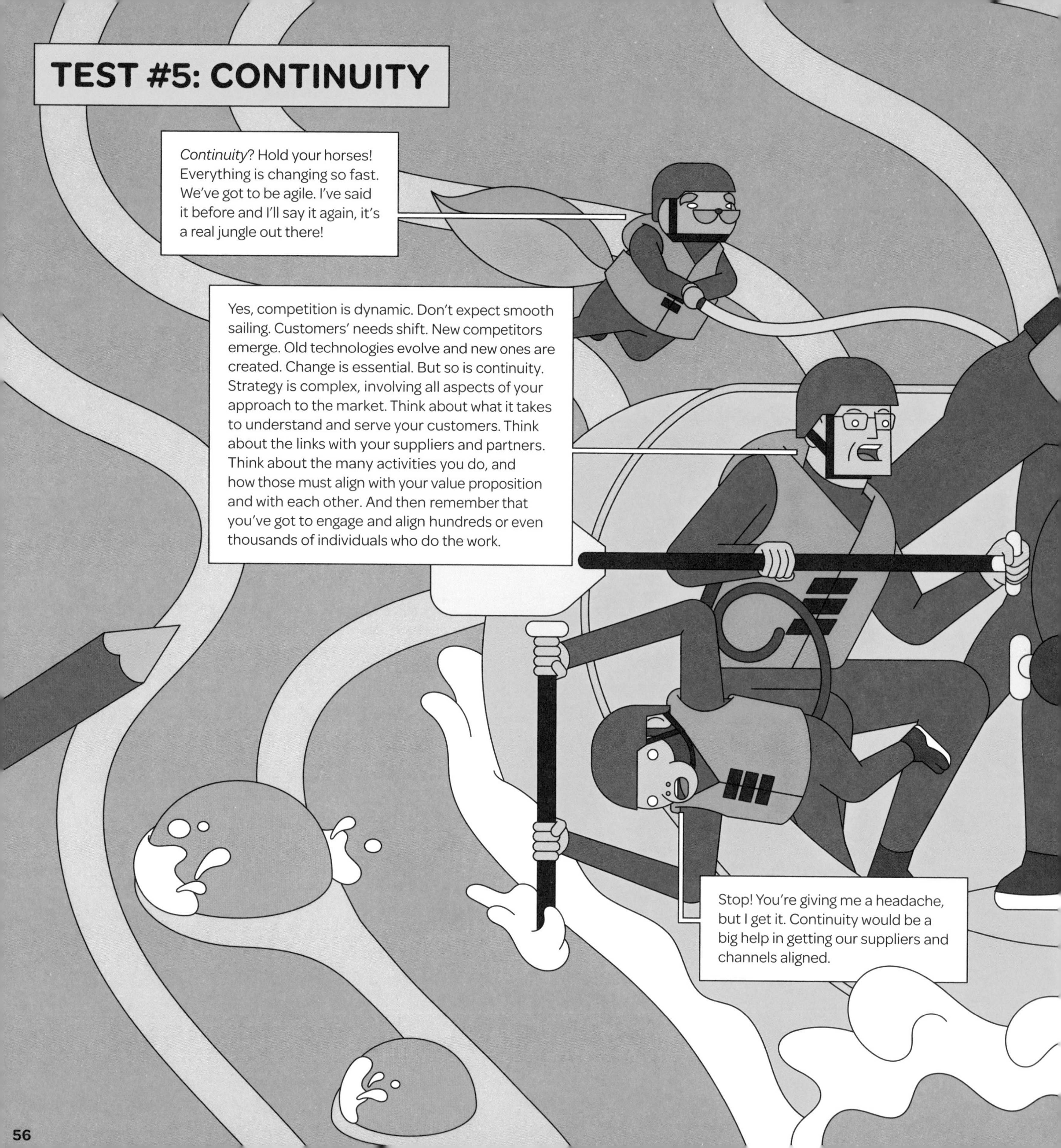
Continuity? Hold your horses! Everything is changing so fast. We've got to be agile. I've said it before and I'll say it again, it's a real jungle out there!
Yes, competition is dynamic. Don't expect smooth sailing. Customers' needs shift. New competitors emerge. Old technologies evolve and new ones are created. Change is essential. But so is continuity. Strategy is complex, involving all aspects of your approach to the market. Think about what it takes to understand and serve your customers. Think about the links with your suppliers and partners. Think about the many activities you do, and how those must align with your value proposition and with each other. And then remember that you've got to engage and align hundreds or even thousands of individuals who do the work.
Stop! You're giving me a headache, but I get it. Continuity would be a big help in getting our suppliers and channels aligned.

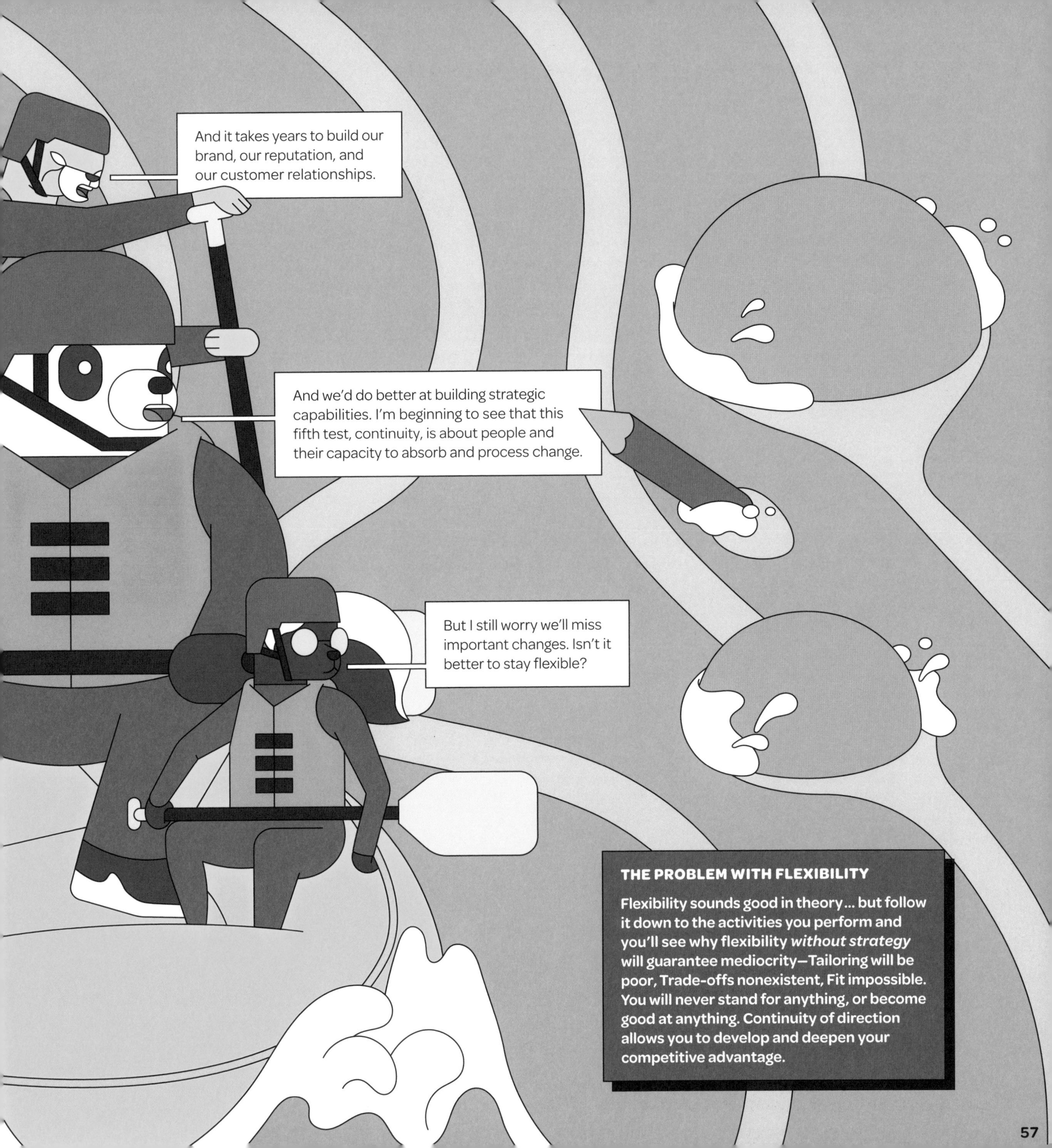
And it takes years to build our brand, our reputation, and our customer relationships.
And we'd do better at building strategic capabilities. I'm beginning to see that this fifth test, continuity, is about people and their capacity to absorb and process change.
But I still worry we'll miss important changes. Isn't it better to stay flexible?

THE PROBLEM WITH FLEXIBILITY

Flexibility sounds good in theory… but follow it down to the activities you perform and you'll see why flexibility *without strategy* will guarantee mediocrity—Tailoring will be poor, Trade-offs nonexistent, Fit impossible. You will never stand for anything, or become good at anything. Continuity of direction allows you to develop and deepen your competitive advantage.

TEST #5: CONTINUITY AND DISRUPTION

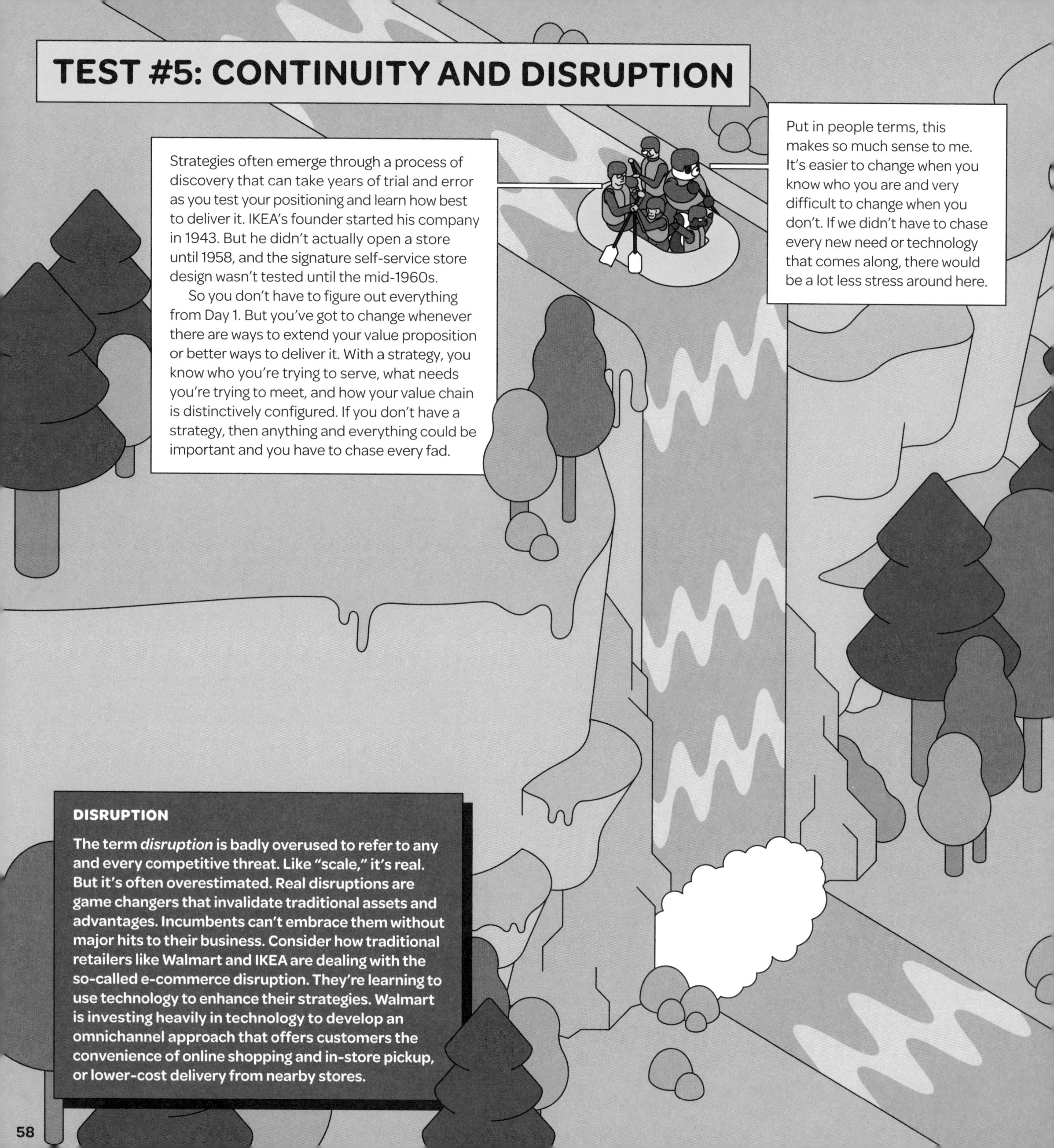

Strategies often emerge through a process of discovery that can take years of trial and error as you test your positioning and learn how best to deliver it. IKEA's founder started his company in 1943. But he didn't actually open a store until 1958, and the signature self-service store design wasn't tested until the mid-1960s.

So you don't have to figure out everything from Day 1. But you've got to change whenever there are ways to extend your value proposition or better ways to deliver it. With a strategy, you know who you're trying to serve, what needs you're trying to meet, and how your value chain is distinctively configured. If you don't have a strategy, then anything and everything could be important and you have to chase every fad.

Put in people terms, this makes so much sense to me. It's easier to change when you know who you are and very difficult to change when you don't. If we didn't have to chase every new need or technology that comes along, there would be a lot less stress around here.

DISRUPTION

The term *disruption* is badly overused to refer to any and every competitive threat. Like "scale," it's real. But it's often overestimated. Real disruptions are game changers that invalidate traditional assets and advantages. Incumbents can't embrace them without major hits to their business. Consider how traditional retailers like Walmart and IKEA are dealing with the so-called e-commerce disruption. They're learning to use technology to enhance their strategies. Walmart is investing heavily in technology to develop an omnichannel approach that offers customers the convenience of online shopping and in-store pickup, or lower-cost delivery from nearby stores.

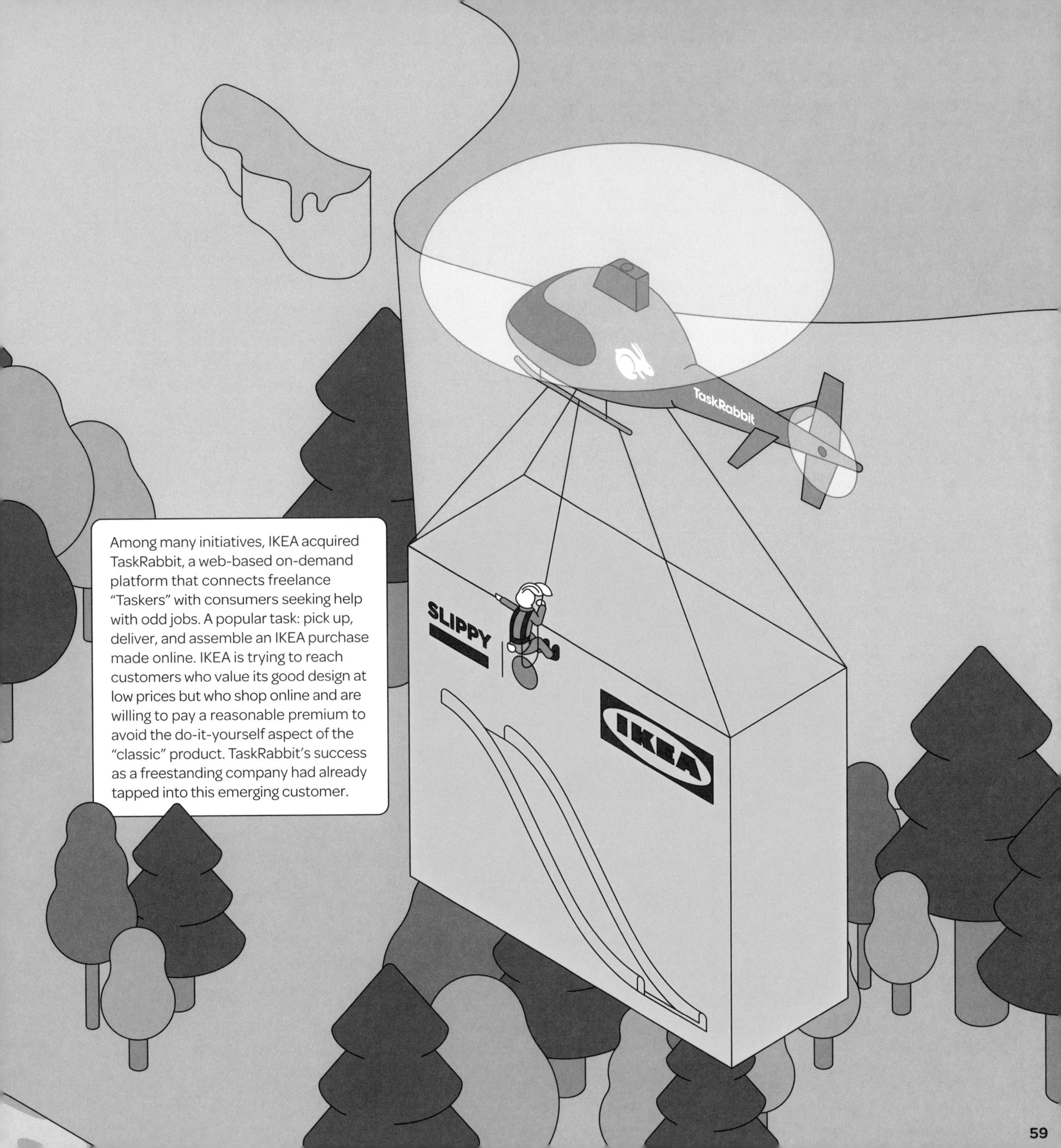
TaskRabbit
SLIPPY
IKEA

Among many initiatives, IKEA acquired TaskRabbit, a web-based on-demand platform that connects freelance "Taskers" with consumers seeking help with odd jobs. A popular task: pick up, deliver, and assemble an IKEA purchase made online. IKEA is trying to reach customers who value its good design at low prices but who shop online and are willing to pay a reasonable premium to avoid the do-it-yourself aspect of the "classic" product. TaskRabbit's success as a freestanding company had already tapped into this emerging customer.

TEST #5: CONTINUITY AND INNOVATION

Disruption calls for a more rigorous and analytic approach. How does the innovation impact the value chain? The value proposition? Relative price? Relative cost? Apply the strategy fundamentals. Is the change disruptive, or is it a new best practice everyone must embrace? Can it be used to reinforce your strategy without compromising its uniqueness?

Many new technologies—even big leaps—are not disruptive. That certainly was true for the internet. Companies figure out how to absorb new technologies, and then they move on.

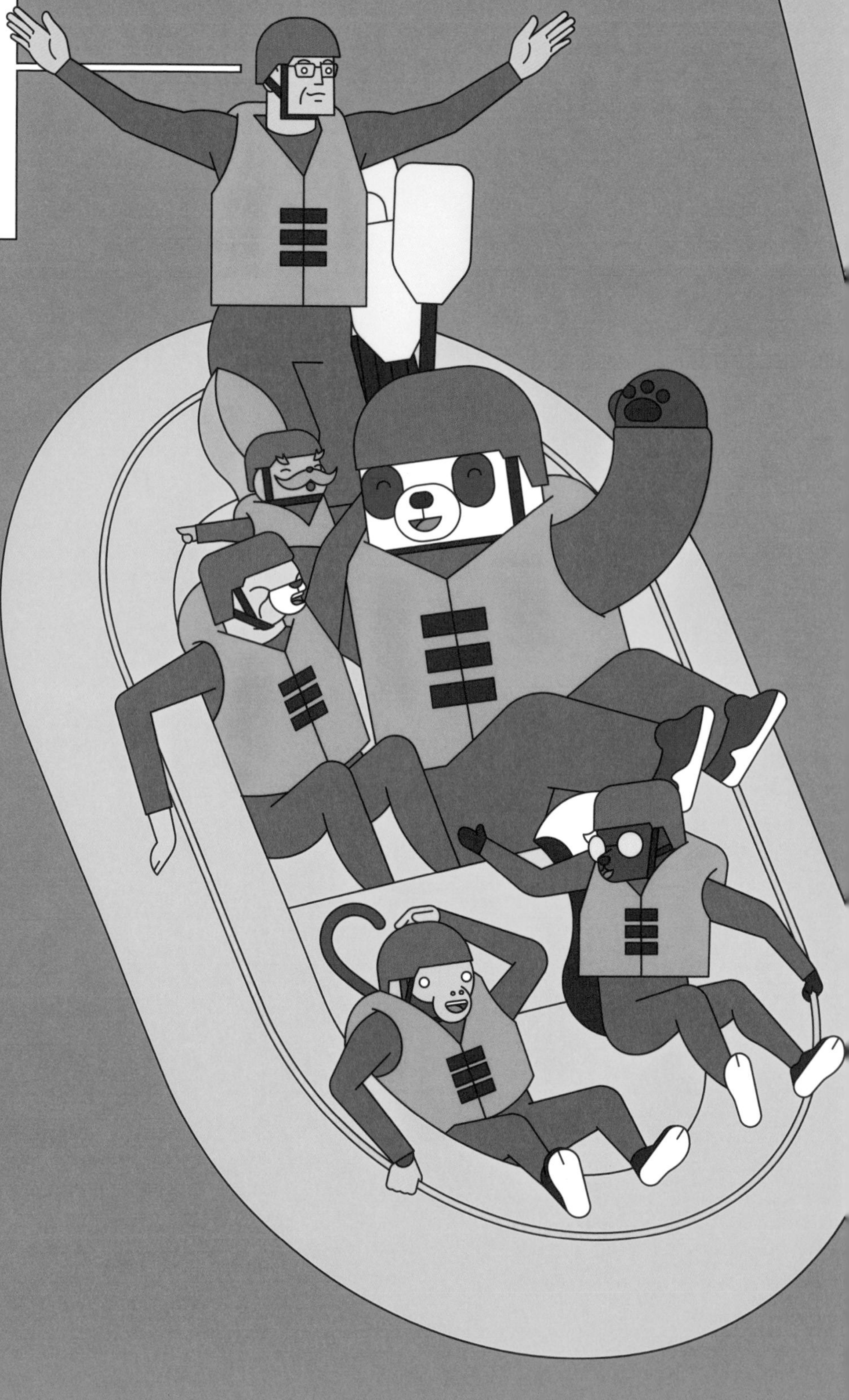

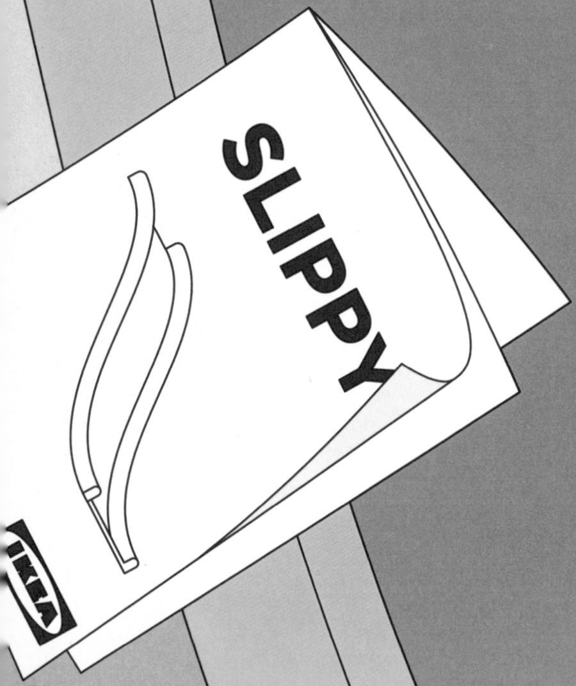
SLIPPY

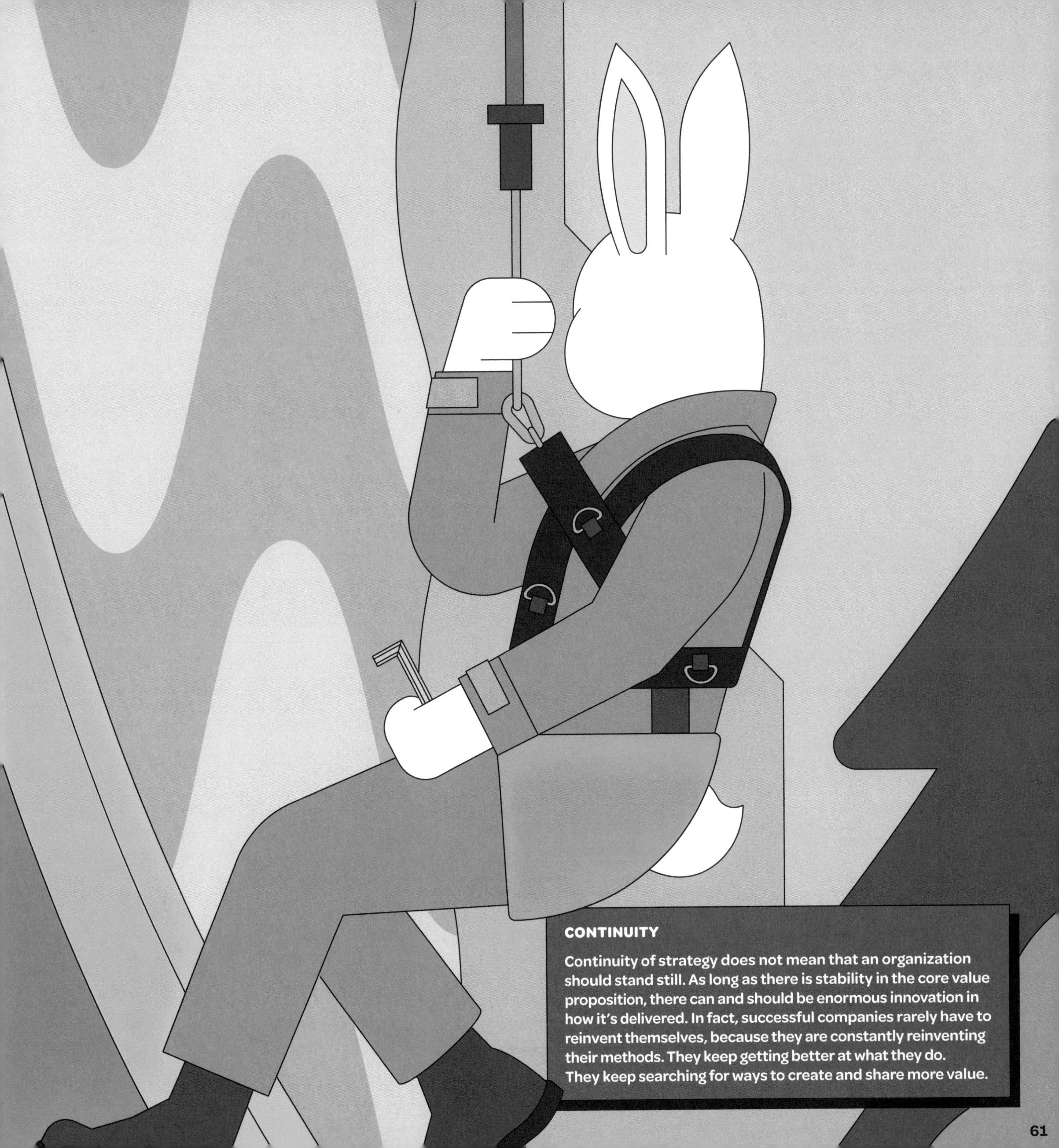

CONTINUITY

Continuity of strategy does not mean that an organization should stand still. As long as there is stability in the core value proposition, there can and should be enormous innovation in how it's delivered. In fact, successful companies rarely have to reinvent themselves, because they are constantly reinventing their methods. They keep getting better at what they do. They keep searching for ways to create and share more value.

BUT CAN COMPETITIVE ADVANTAGES BE SUSTAINED?

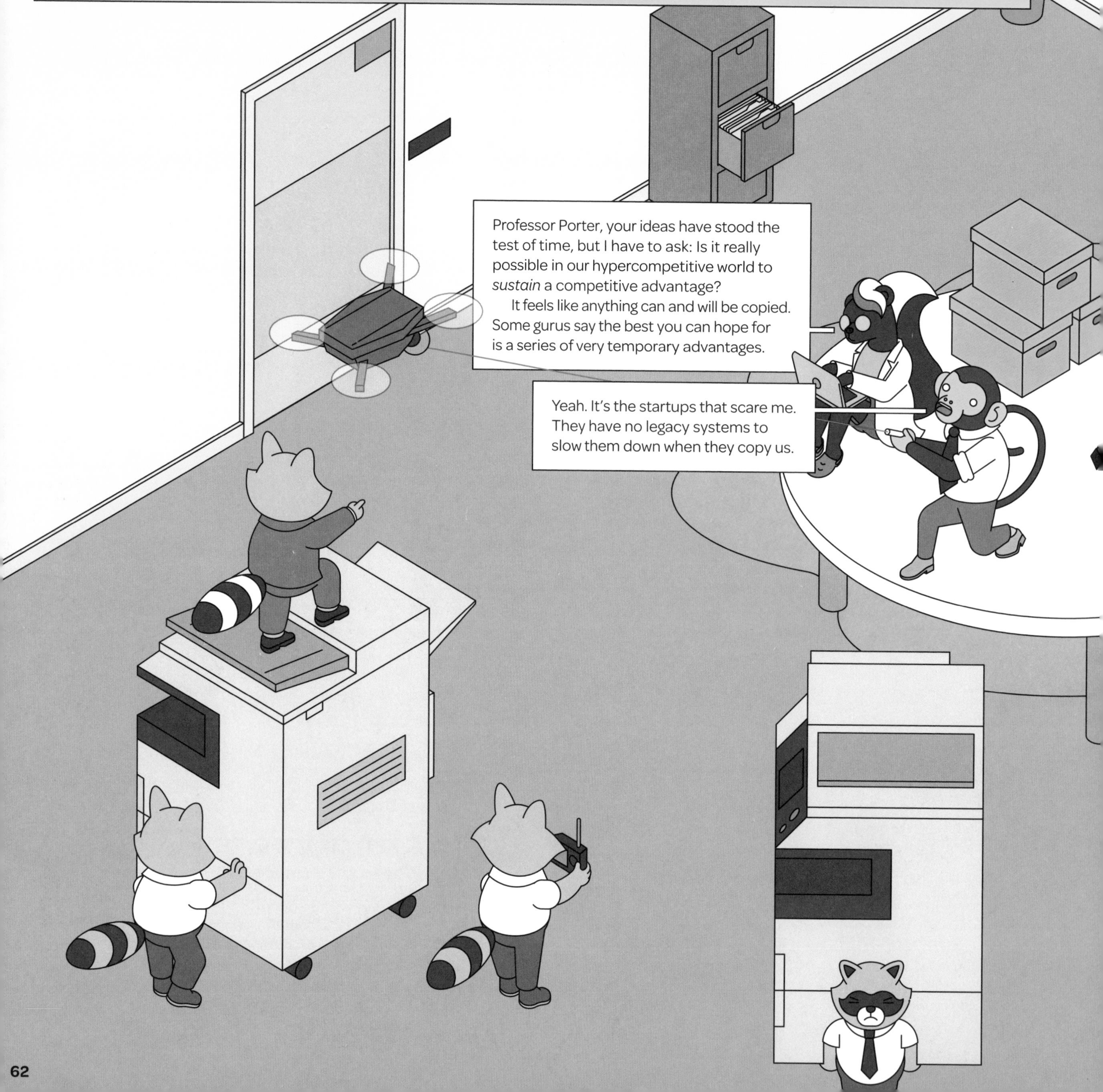
Professor Porter, your ideas have stood the test of time, but I have to ask: Is it really possible in our hypercompetitive world to *sustain* a competitive advantage?
It feels like anything can and will be copied. Some gurus say the best you can hope for is a series of very temporary advantages.
Yeah. It's the startups that scare me. They have no legacy systems to slow them down when they copy us.

No doubt if you are successful, someone will try to copy you. But remember my tests. A tailored value chain—*different activities*—is the first line of defense against imitation. Trade-offs provide even stronger economic barriers to copycats. The more activities existing rivals have to reconfigure, the more they will damage their own current positions. And fit can deter even the most determined new entrants. To succeed, they've got to copy a whole nest of interdependent activities, mostly invisible to outsiders. Even if they could figure it out, replicating all of it would involve hundreds of integrated decisions that cross organizational lines. That's really hard.

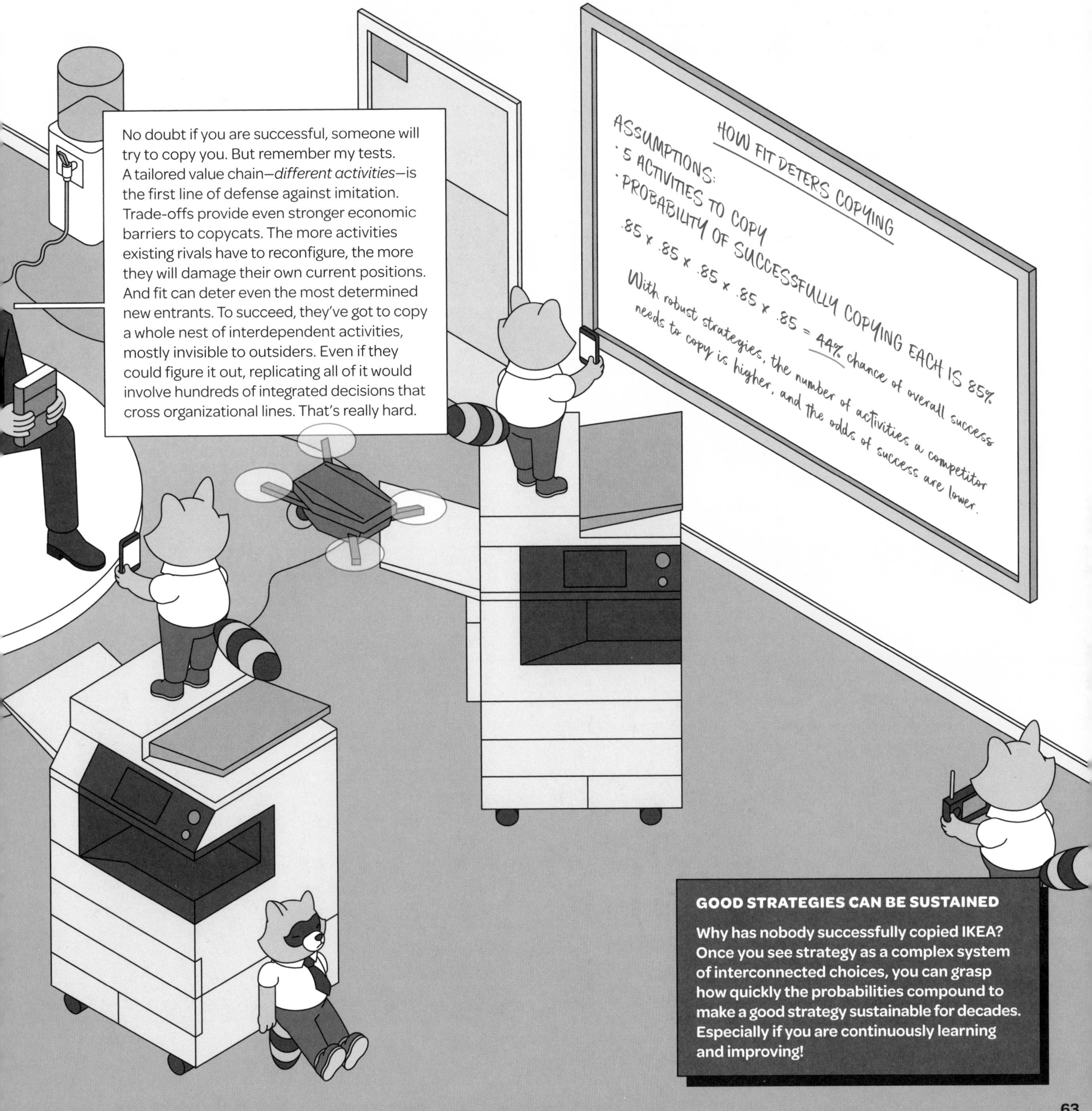

HOW FIT DETERS COPYING
ASSUMPTIONS:
· 5 ACTIVITIES TO COPY
· PROBABILITY OF SUCCESSFULLY COPYING EACH IS 85%
.85 x .85 x .85 x .85 x .85 = 44% chance of overall success
With robust strategies, the number of activities a competitor needs to copy is higher, and the odds of success are lower.

GOOD STRATEGIES CAN BE SUSTAINED

Why has nobody successfully copied IKEA? Once you see strategy as a complex system of interconnected choices, you can grasp how quickly the probabilities compound to make a good strategy sustainable for decades. Especially if you are continuously learning and improving!

WRAPPING UP: A STRATEGY CHECKLIST

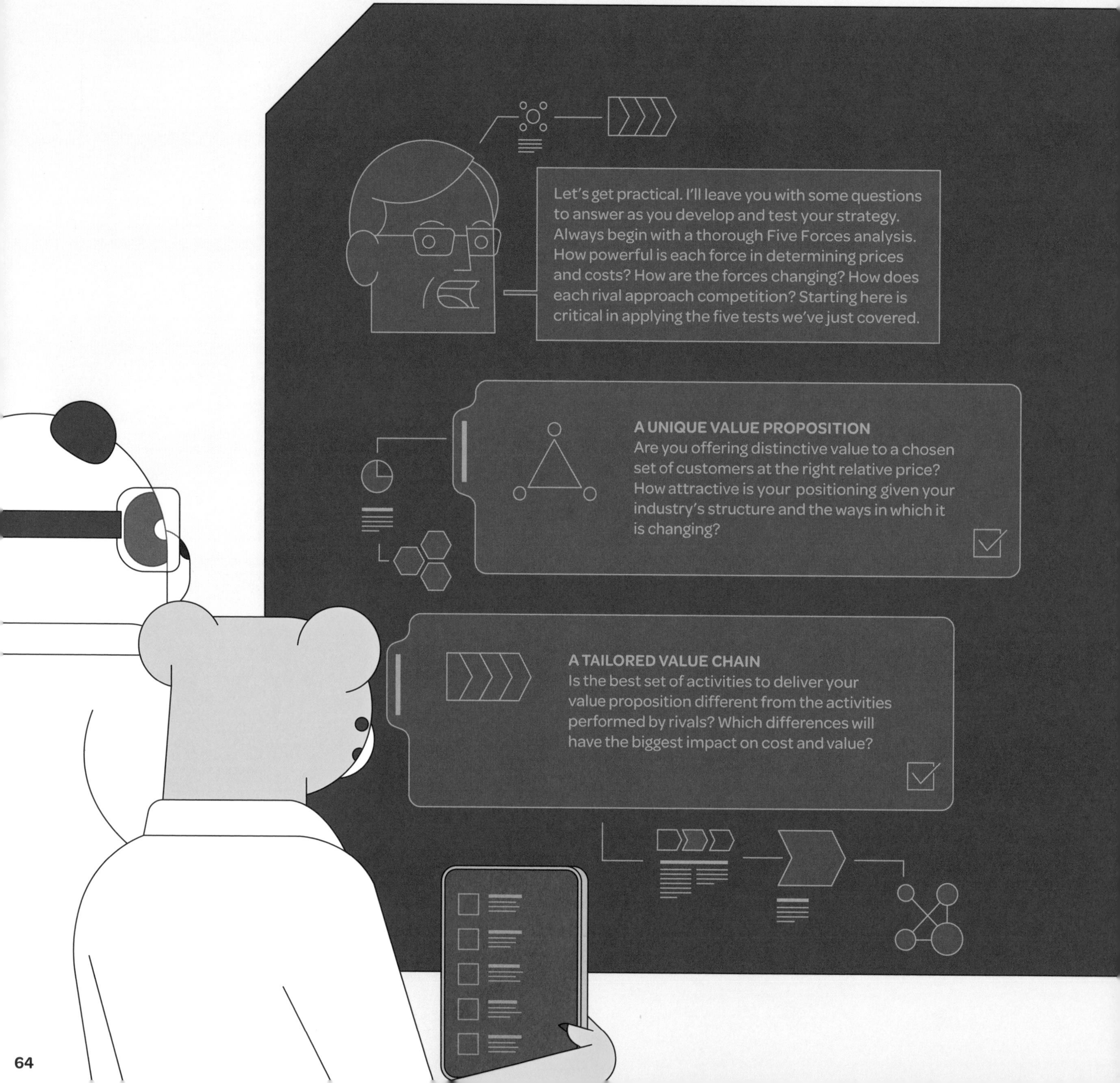

Let's get practical. I'll leave you with some questions to answer as you develop and test your strategy. Always begin with a thorough Five Forces analysis. How powerful is each force in determining prices and costs? How are the forces changing? How does each rival approach competition? Starting here is critical in applying the five tests we've just covered.

A UNIQUE VALUE PROPOSITION
Are you offering distinctive value to a chosen set of customers at the right relative price? How attractive is your positioning given your industry's structure and the ways in which it is changing?

A TAILORED VALUE CHAIN
Is the best set of activities to deliver your value proposition different from the activities performed by rivals? Which differences will have the biggest impact on cost and value?

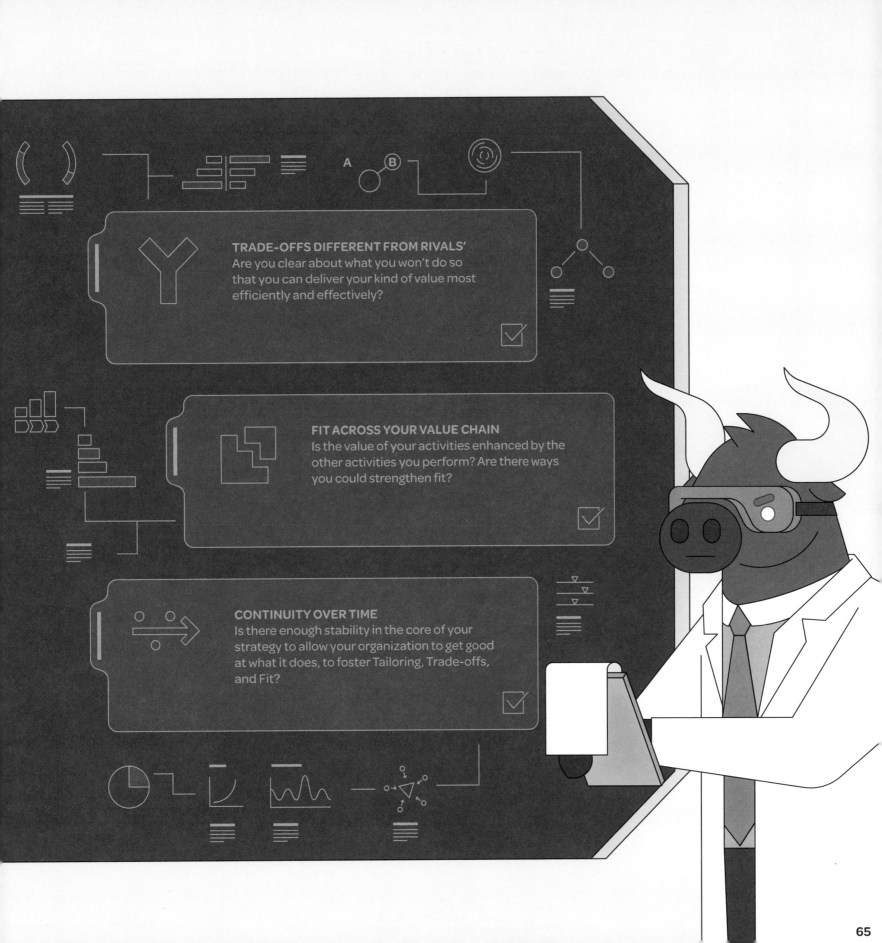

TRADE-OFFS DIFFERENT FROM RIVALS'
Are you clear about what you won't do so that you can deliver your kind of value most efficiently and effectively?

FIT ACROSS YOUR VALUE CHAIN
Is the value of your activities enhanced by the other activities you perform? Are there ways you could strengthen fit?

CONTINUITY OVER TIME
Is there enough stability in the core of your strategy to allow your organization to get good at what it does, to foster Tailoring, Trade-offs, and Fit?

COMMON STRATEGY MISTAKES

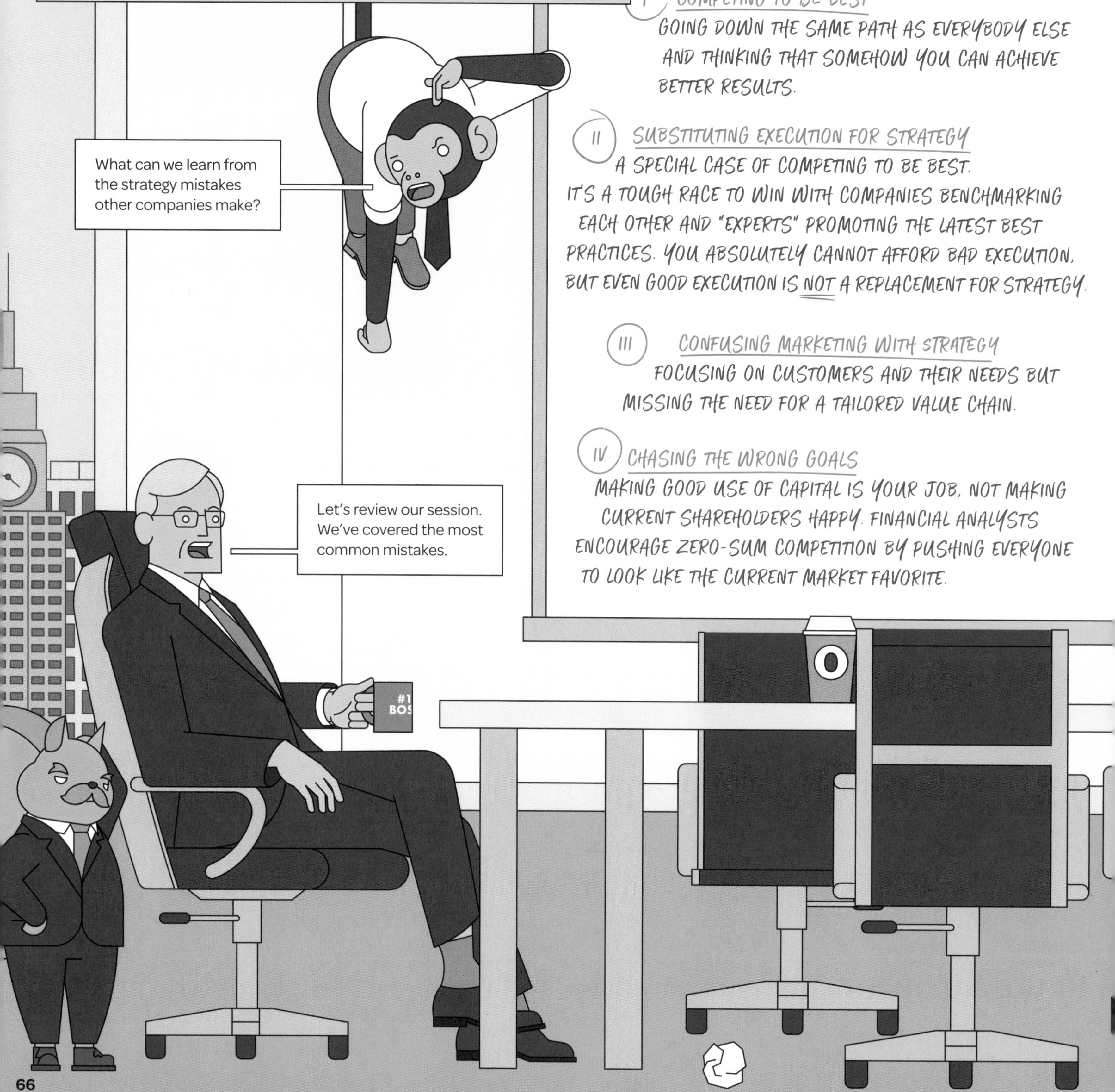

I COMPETING TO BE BEST
GOING DOWN THE SAME PATH AS EVERYBODY ELSE AND THINKING THAT SOMEHOW YOU CAN ACHIEVE BETTER RESULTS.
II SUBSTITUTING EXECUTION FOR STRATEGY
A SPECIAL CASE OF COMPETING TO BE BEST.
IT'S A TOUGH RACE TO WIN WITH COMPANIES BENCHMARKING EACH OTHER AND "EXPERTS" PROMOTING THE LATEST BEST PRACTICES. YOU ABSOLUTELY CANNOT AFFORD BAD EXECUTION, BUT EVEN GOOD EXECUTION IS NOT A REPLACEMENT FOR STRATEGY.
III CONFUSING MARKETING WITH STRATEGY
FOCUSING ON CUSTOMERS AND THEIR NEEDS BUT MISSING THE NEED FOR A TAILORED VALUE CHAIN.
IV CHASING THE WRONG GOALS
MAKING GOOD USE OF CAPITAL IS YOUR JOB, NOT MAKING CURRENT SHAREHOLDERS HAPPY. FINANCIAL ANALYSTS ENCOURAGE ZERO-SUM COMPETITION BY PUSHING EVERYONE TO LOOK LIKE THE CURRENT MARKET FAVORITE.
What can we learn from the strategy mistakes other companies make?
Let's review our session. We've covered the most common mistakes.

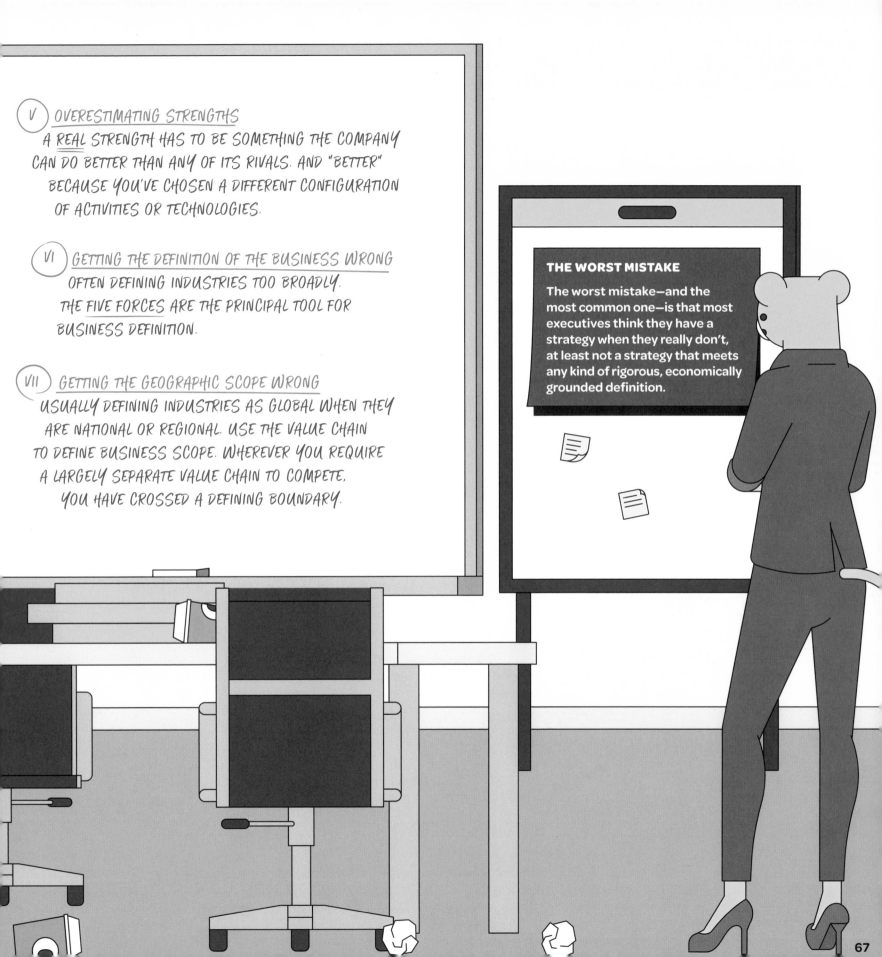

V OVERESTIMATING STRENGTHS
A REAL STRENGTH HAS TO BE SOMETHING THE COMPANY
CAN DO BETTER THAN ANY OF ITS RIVALS. AND "BETTER"
BECAUSE YOU'VE CHOSEN A DIFFERENT CONFIGURATION
OF ACTIVITIES OR TECHNOLOGIES.

VI GETTING THE DEFINITION OF THE BUSINESS WRONG
OFTEN DEFINING INDUSTRIES TOO BROADLY.
THE FIVE FORCES ARE THE PRINCIPAL TOOL FOR
BUSINESS DEFINITION.

VII GETTING THE GEOGRAPHIC SCOPE WRONG
USUALLY DEFINING INDUSTRIES AS GLOBAL WHEN THEY
ARE NATIONAL OR REGIONAL. USE THE VALUE CHAIN
TO DEFINE BUSINESS SCOPE. WHEREVER YOU REQUIRE
A LARGELY SEPARATE VALUE CHAIN TO COMPETE,
YOU HAVE CROSSED A DEFINING BOUNDARY.

THE WORST MISTAKE

The worst mistake—and the most common one—is that most executives think they have a strategy when they really don't, at least not a strategy that meets any kind of rigorous, economically grounded definition.

THERE'S MORE TO LEARN...

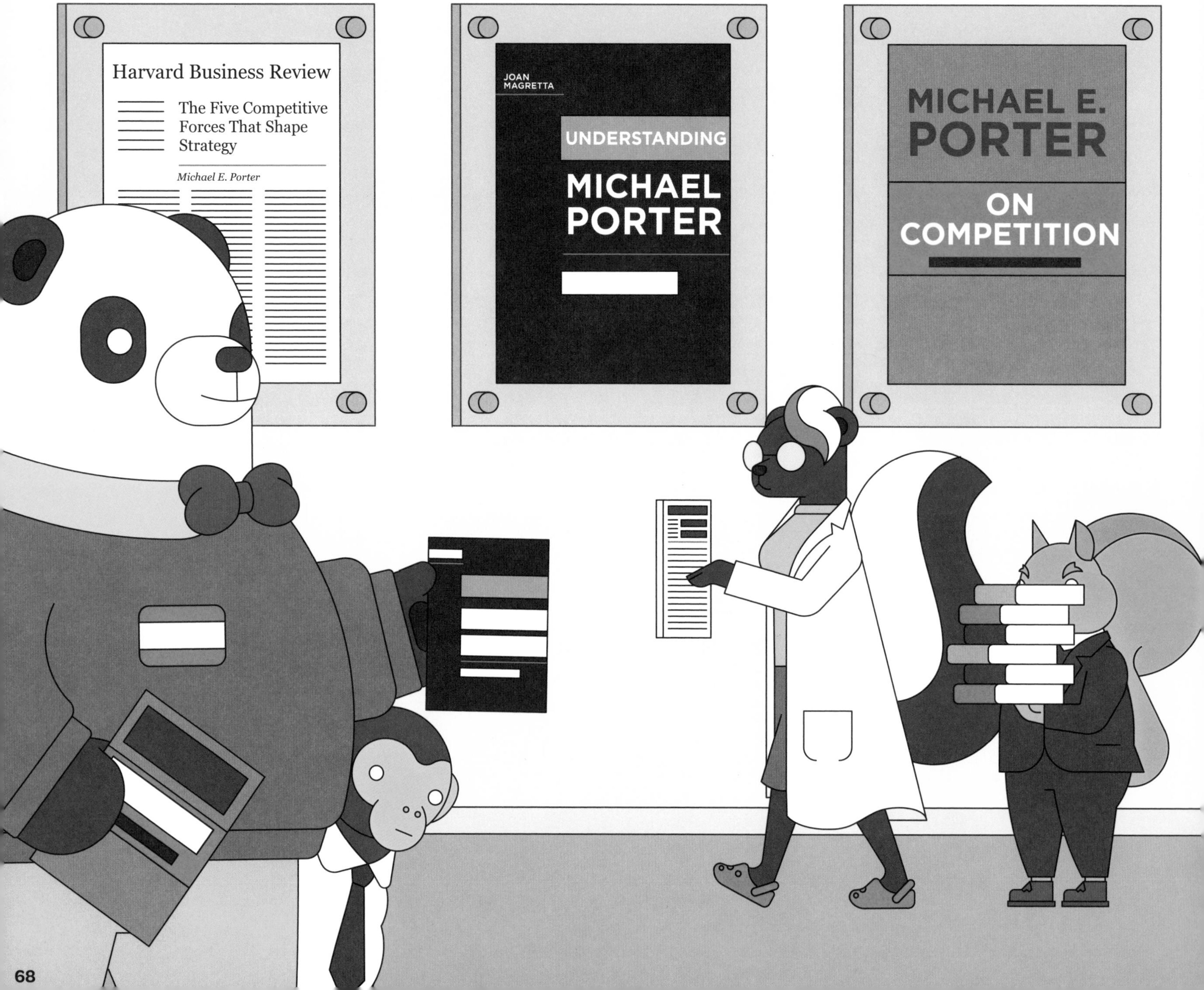
Harvard Business Review
The Five Competitive Forces That Shape Strategy
Michael E. Porter
JOAN MAGRETTA
UNDERSTANDING
MICHAEL PORTER
MICHAEL E. PORTER
ON COMPETITION

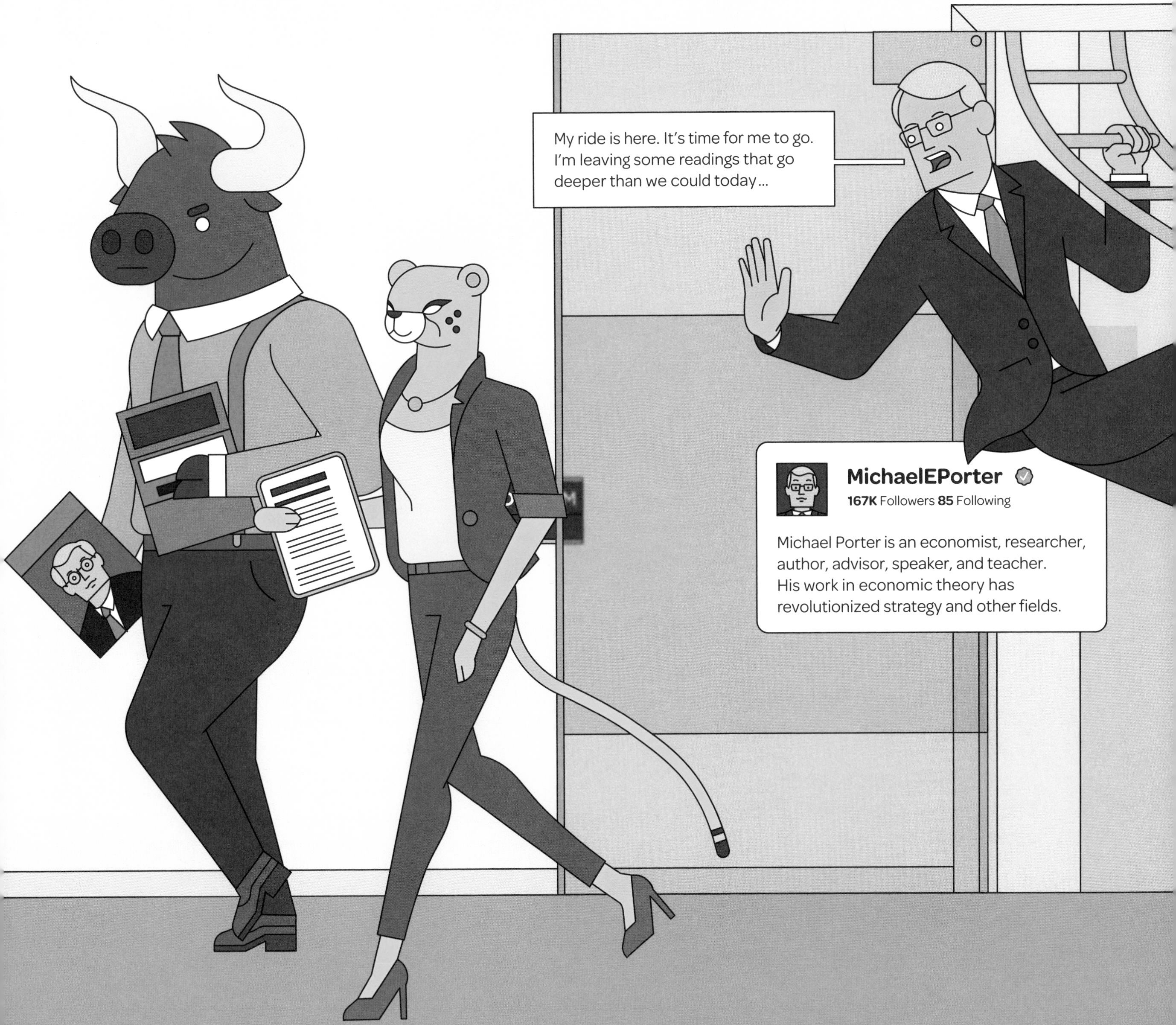
My ride is here. It's time for me to go.
I'm leaving some readings that go
deeper than we could today...
MichaelEPorter
167K Followers 85 Following
Michael Porter is an economist, researcher,
author, advisor, speaker, and teacher.
His work in economic theory has
revolutionized strategy and other fields.

GLOSSARY-INDEX OF CORE CONCEPTS

Business Definition (28, 67)
An industry is a set of players who share the same basic Five Forces. Where there are differences in more than one force, or where differences in any one force are large, you are likely dealing with distinct industries. Each will need its own strategy.

Competing to Be the Best (14, 66)
A race to the bottom that no one can win, unleashed when companies compete head-to-head on the same dimensions.

Competing to Be Unique (15)
A positive-sum form of rivalry focused on creating unique value for chosen customers, not on beating rivals. Potential for multiple winners.

Competitive Advantage (32–37, 62–63)
A term often used loosely, but Porter's definition is precise. You have a competitive advantage if your profitability is sustainably higher than that of your rivals. That means you operate at a lower cost, command a premium price, or both. It's simple math—the only way to generate superior profits—and it comes from doing unique things or doing similar things in unique ways.

Competitive Strategy (12–13)
The set of integrated choices that define how you will outperform your industry in the face of competition.

Continuity (56–61, 65)
Continuity of direction allows a company to develop the elements of its strategy and to deepen its competitive advantage. As long as there is stability in the core value proposition, there can and should be enormous innovation in how it's delivered.

Corporate Strategy (12–13)
The overall strategy for a corporation that consists of diversified businesses competing in multiple businesses. It is not the same thing as a competitive strategy.

Disruption (58–61)
A term overused to refer to any and every competitive threat. Real disruptions are game changers that invalidate traditional assets and advantages. Many feared "disruptions" turn out to be new best practices incumbents must embrace. Real disruptions can be identified rigorously by applying the strategy fundamentals.

Fit (50–55, 63, 65)
Occurs when the value or cost of one activity is affected by the way other activities are performed. Good strategies don't rely on just one thing, on making one choice, but on the connection among many interdependent choices. Fit can amplify the value of a competitive advantage by lowering costs or by justifying higher relative prices.

Five Forces (22–27)
The tug-of-war among rivals, customers, suppliers, substitutes, and potential new entrants that determines the average prices and costs in that industry. Insights about industry structure gained from a Five Forces analysis should lead directly to decisions about where and how to compete.

Industry Structure (21–27, 29)
The basic, underlying economic and technological characteristics of an industry that shape the competitive arena in which strategy must be set. Collectively, the Five Forces determine the structure of an industry.

Positive-Sum Competition (15)
A form of competition in which there can be multiple winners. See "Competing to Be Unique."

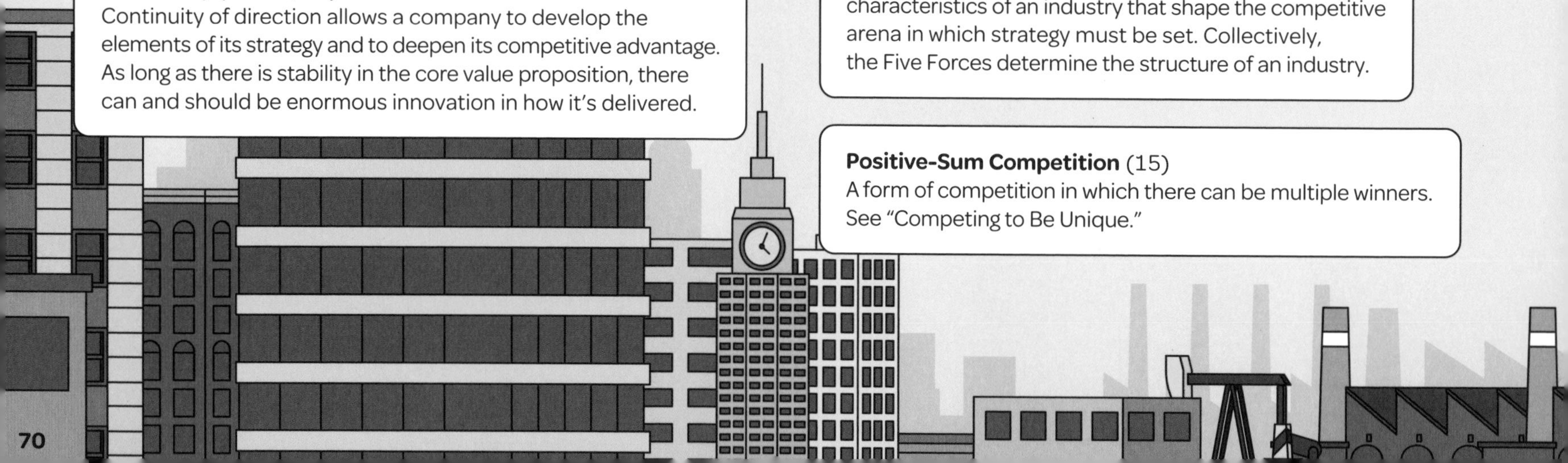

Return on Invested Capital (ROIC) (20–21)
The most reliable goal for strategy. It weighs the profits a business generates against the capital invested in it. Superior ROIC—sustainable over years, not just in the next quarter—tells you you're creating value *and* making good use of capital.

Scale (16)
How big do you have to be? Scale advantages can be important in competition, but they are often overestimated. You don't have to dominate as long as you are big enough for your chosen strategy.

Strategic Positioning (21, 27)
The choice of a value proposition made against a specific and relevant set of industry rivals. Discovering a good strategy means finding a unique positioning, the "place" you want to be in your industry. See also "Unique Value Proposition."

Sustainability of Strategy (62–63)
The ability to maintain a competitive advantage when faced with existing rivals and new entrants who try to copy your strategy. Tailoring, trade-offs, and fit are powerful deterrents to would-be imitators.

Tailored Value Chain (43–45, 54–55, 62–63, 64)
Robust strategies always involve a significant degree of tailoring choices to perform activities differently or to perform different activities than rivals in order to deliver most effectively an organization's unique value proposition. Tailoring provides the economic basis for superior profitability.

Trade-offs (46–49, 54–55, 62–63, 65)
Making trade-offs means saying no to some customers, products, or services to better deliver others. A trade-off—whether in the product itself or in how you produce and sell it—means that you can't have it both ways, because the choices are incompatible. You've got to choose, or else accept mediocre performance.

Unique Value Proposition (39–42, 64)
The core element of strategy that determines a strategic positioning. It defines the kind of value a company will create for its customers by answering three questions: Which customers will you serve? Which needs will you meet? And at what relative price? If your value proposition is not different from your rivals', you're competing to be the best.

Value Chain (34–37, 43–45)
A map of the operational activities a company performs to design, produce, sell, deliver, and support its products. This is the basic tool for understanding the sources of competitive advantage—the specific activities that result in premium prices or lower costs.

Value System (35–37)
The full set of end-to-end activities involved in creating value for the end user regardless of who performs them. A company's value chain is typically just a part of a larger value system that includes companies either upstream (suppliers) or downstream (distribution channels), or both.

Zero-Sum Competition (14)
A form of competition in which one player's gain is another's loss. See "Competing to Be the Best."

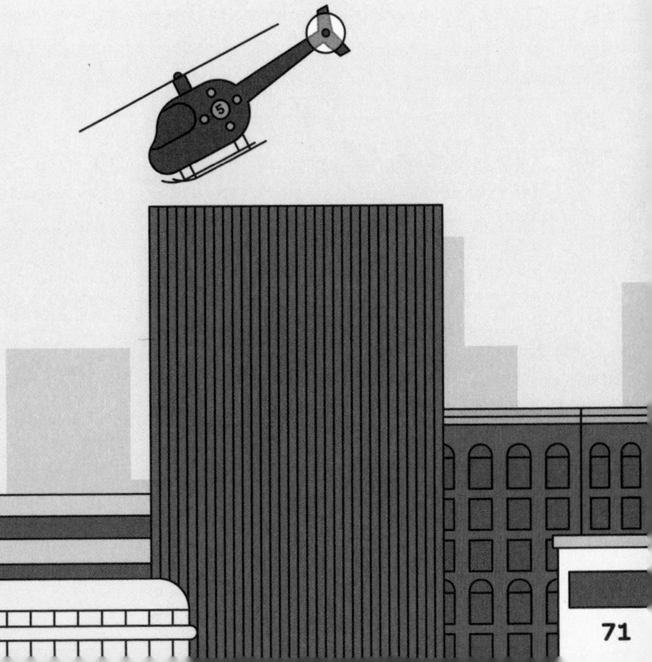

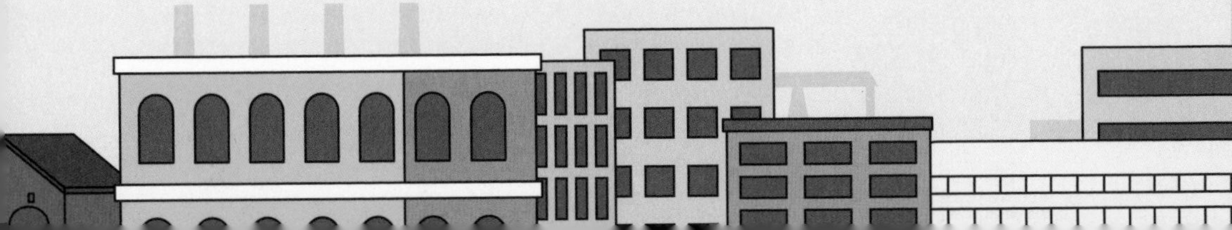

About Our Team

Joan Magretta has worked with Michael Porter for over two decades. She is a senior associate at the Institute for Strategy and Competitiveness at Harvard Business School, a McKinsey Award winner, and the author of the bestselling books *Understanding Michael Porter* and *What Management Is*, the latter a top pick by the *Economist* when it was first published. Previously, she was a Bain partner and a strategy editor at *Harvard Business Review*.

Emile Holmewood is an award-winning illustrator and animator. A New Zealander, he is currently based in Tokyo after building an advertising and editorial reputation in London. His work has appeared in leading global publications, from the *New York Times* to London's *Guardian* and *Observer*, and in public spaces like Madison Square Garden. Among his advertising clients have been Apple and Bank of America. Emile's illustrations are informed by his background in graphic design. He is a master of transforming complex ideas into humorous images.

Heinrich Zimmermann is a partner at a strategy consultancy based in Frankfurt and Tel Aviv. He was a founding partner of the Institute for New Communication, an interdisciplinary think tank and design lab based in Germany. He originated the concept for this book and assembled the team to turn his vision into reality.

Acknowledgments

This book could not have happened without the support of Michael Porter, who graciously allowed us to use his image in ways he could never have imagined when he gave us carte blanche. His reviews of our text, always instructive, guided us in our mission to present his thinking clearly and concisely without dumbing it down.

Thanks also to Rafe Sagalyn, whose early guidance was essential, and to Paula Duffy, for her wise counsel about every aspect of this book from start to finish. This is a better book thanks to the keen, professional eye of Nikolas Brückmann, who created the layout and typography. And finally, we are grateful to our editor, Melinda Merino, who championed this unconventional project from the beginning and who, along with Design Director Stephani Finks, challenged us in all the right ways.

Printed in the United States of America
10 9 8 7 6 5 4 3 2 1

Library of Congress Cataloging-in-Publication Data is forthcoming.
ISBN: 978-1-63369-823-9
eISBN: 978-1-63369-824-6

The paper used in this publication meets the requirements of the American National Standard for Permanence of Paper for Publications and Documents in Libraries and Archives Z39.48-1992.

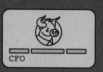